PLAYTIME
FOR YOUR DOG

PLAYTIME
FOR YOUR DOG

Keep him busy
throughout the day

by Christina Sondermann

We would like to thank all the two- and four-legged helpers that have contributed to the development and the success of this book: whether through their commitment during our photo sessions, through constructive proof reading or by telling us their inspiring ideas on playing with dogs!
I hope that by having this book translated, even more people and dogs all over the world will be infected with game fever. Of course, I'm also curious: what kind of games are you playing with your dogs? How do you take care of variety in your dog's everyday life? Please send me your firsthand reports, game ideas, words, pictures and also any links on playing with dogs! I'm looking forward to your emails!

Christina Sondermann, Meschede/Germany, February 2006

Info@fun-with-dogs.com
www.fun-with-dogs.com

Copyright of German edition: © 2005 by Cadmos Verlag GmbH, Brunsbek
Copyright of this edition: © 2006/2009 by Cadmos Equestrian
Arrangement and setting: Ravenstein and Partners, Verden
Photos: Christina Sondermann
Printing: Westermann, Zwickau

Printed in Germany

ISBN 978-3-86127-922-8

Table of contents

Why playing is so useful 10

Rules of the game and tips for beginners 14
   The right game for you and your dog 14
   Rewards are the key to success 15
   Food works best 16
   Step-by-step to success 16
   Accurate timing 19
   Helpful training assistants 19
   Keep it simple and easy 20
   What if it doesn't work? 20
   Your dog is the best indicator of good mood 21
   When children are participating 22
   How to manage the multi-dog household 22

Sniffing games for super-noses 25
   Beginners' class 26
      Searching for a meal 27
      Hidden treats 27
      Search-work in the dark 28
      Treats hidden in a pile of blankets 28
      The sniffing box 28
      Take a plunge 28
      Searching the three dimensions 29
      Laying a scent track 29
      Toys instead of treats 29
      You want even more? 30
   Scent discrimination the easy way 31
      The shell game 31
      Sniffing for professionals 32
   Quick introduction into tracking 35

Living room agility 38

Various fantasy obstacles 39
The curtain 39
The dog flap 40
Weave poles and mobility games 40
Living room obstacles for high achievers 41
Never-ending tunnels and tubes 41
The collapsed tunnel adventure 42
Hoops and other openings 43
Challenges on the ground 44
Co-ordination exercises with a ladder 45
Balancing on a wobble board 46
Climbing tours 46
Crazy labyrinths 47
The 101 things game 47
101 things to do with a chair 47
101 things to do with a chair for the experienced 48
More 101 things adventures 48
Gymnastics 48
Sitting down 49
Flat on your belly ... or your back 49
On all fours 49
Standing 49
Using your arms 49

Mental exercise – Challenges for bright young sparks 50

Exercises for package artists 51
Fascinating cardboard boxes 51
Cardboard box mountain 51
Box in a box 52
Special packages 53
Tupperware party for our four-legged friends 54
What's next? 54

Just staggering 55
   Treats under bowls 55
   Flower pot challenge 55
   Treats under the flower pot roller board 56
   A game of chance under cups 57
   Treat bowling 58
Think outside the box 58
   Skilful paws 58
   A fishing rod for your dog 59
   The treat box 59
   Punch and Judy show 60
Intelligent machines 61
   Spin the bottle 61
   The drawer 62
   The down-pipe 64
   Sitting in front of the pipe 67
Treat balls and other food dispensers 69
   The food bottle 70
   A filled tube 71
   Classical treat balls 71
   The cube 72
   The food skipjack 73
Games to buy for mental acrobats 73

Chewing makes you happy! 75
   Chewing objects as they are! 77
   Natural rubber toys 78
   Snacks and packed lunch 81

Having fun with "Sit" – "Down" – "Come" 84
   For starters, create the right spirit 85
   Coming back is fun! 85

Who is calling best? 87
Back and forth variations 87
Come and find me! 88
Coming back game for singles 89
The treat lane 89
The flying dog 91
"Sit" and "down" in different places 91
Strange positions 92
"Sit" and "down" criss-cross 94
"Sit" and "down" everywhere! 95
Staying power 96
Building bridges 97
The loose lead 98
The fine cord 98
Egg-and-spoon race 99

Your garden as a playground .100
Space for high jumps 102
Basic jumps 102
Self-made professional jumps 102
Jumps as tests of courage 104
Weave poles 104
Basic weave poles 104
Do-it-yourself professional weave poles 105
More mobility exercises 105
Tunnels and hoops 105
Living obstacles 107
Tests of courage and co-ordination games 108
Fantasy obstacles for body awareness training 108
The fumble course 109
The dog teeter 109
Rolling adventure 110

Water games 112
The digging corner 112
The mixed course 113
Anything else? 113

Adventure walks - looking for Ideas on the way 114
Open air course along the way 115
Balancing act 116
Platforms and other climbing opportunities 116
Higgledy-piggledy! 117
Co-ordination exercises on your way 118
Round and round it goes 118
Adventures at the waterside 119
Bathing challenge 119
Treat tracing 120
Bridges and catwalks 120
Rummaging and searching games 120
Foraging for treats 121
Hide and seek 121
Sniffing walks 122
Sniffing and exploring 122
Sniffing in a group is even more fun 124

And what comes next? 125

Recommended reading 128

Why playing is so useful

You probably have this game book in front of you because you would like to do something with your dog. You would like to offer your four-legged friend something to liven up his daily routine? Perhaps you have already discovered how much fun joint activities are and need more ideas. Then you are in the right place. This book tells you how you can have a lot of fun with your dog, whether at home or on a walk, without needing expensive equipment or complicated training.

You are probably dying to get going already. A wagging tail and a smiling face are really all the encouragement you need to spend time on joint activities and you actually needn't continue reading this chapter. However you will probably enjoy playing even more when you know the positive effects these joint activities can have.

Joint activities liven up your dog's daily routine.

When you give your dog activities to do, you have fewer problems with those he finds for himself.

Playing at home is easy to do and a useful activity that stimulates and satisfies the dog. Bored and under-occupied dogs bite holes in our socks and rip wallpaper off the walls or, in the worst case, they tear the carpet apart. You can prevent this. Joint activities that you can easily integrate into your normal daily routine while away the time and keep your dog happy.

Canine activities are often associated with extensive walks, jogging and bicycle tours or dog sports. Many people (and dogs) also think of throwing and chasing balls and other objects. However it is not always physical exercise that makes an even-tempered dog. Rather, some dogs become wound up by too much action.

And others – due to age, illnesses or size – are hardly in a position for physical exercise. The same can apply to their two-legged partner.

No problem! The possibilities to play at home are so varied, that you can adjust them to the needs of your dog perfectly. If your four-legged friend is a puppy, for instance, then you can stimulate him mentally and encourage his development by using a mixture of brainwork as well as motion and co-ordination games.

You can offer your older dog something as well. Mentally active dogs stay younger longer and many old dogs prove with enthusiasm that they aren't past it yet at all. If your dog is wound up easily and is restless, he can

All dogs like playing – even old dogs or dogs with a handicap: Collie Lana could hardly stand on her feet. Lying on a blanket in the garden she tried out a mental exercise set full of vigour and with sparkling eyes.

learn to concentrate mainly through calm games such as nose-work or brainteasers.

The calmer participants blossom out during living room agility games or on the garden course, and gain self-confidence by passing little tests of courage. And the variety of games possible addresses the tiny Miniature Pinscher as well as the massive Newfoundland.

Overcoming little challenges in the familiar environment of your home builds up your dog's self-confidence. Not only fearful and insecure dogs benefit: when your dog gets used to overcoming little tests of courage or to solving brainwork tasks successfully through playing together, this will also increase his confidence in everyday life. Could there be anything better than an unconcerned, calm dog? He is often less susceptible to problem behaviour and doesn't get out of balance that easily.

When you and your dog are devoted to your play programme within the stress free and distraction free atmosphere of your home and are without any pressure to perform, then you are set up for success. It is not only fun, but almost without realising it, you and your canine companion complete a lesson in dog training at the same time. Along the way, you train yourself by teaching your dog little things. You learn how to motivate him, how he reacts, how you can accelerate his learning process. And your dog also learns through play to understand you better and to interpret your signals and cues.

People who can teach their dogs little tasks or tricks generally have fewer problems with important thing (from a human perspective) like "sit", "down" and "come". The difference between irrelevant and important exercises only exists for us humans, not for the dogs.

The biggest advantage of playing together is the positive effect it has on the relationship between dog and human. It is quite possible that you will get to know and cherish new talents and a fairly new view of your four-legged partner. Your dog will probably experience the same. And both of you will get better and better at communicating with each other. It is likely that your dog will become more altogether attentive and will look out for you to a greater extent – whether at home or on a walk. Maybe, the next time you

Having fun together: playing enriches the relationship between dog and owner.

Is Mum preparing a game there? Meggan certainly doesn't want to miss that!

Little challenges – big effect. Playing together has significantly contributed to Asta – a Beagle rescued from a laboratory – to since becoming a self-confident, happy dog.

call your dog, you will have invented a new activity. And of course Fido will not want to miss that.

To begin your joint play, you need time for your dog (and you should have that as a dog owner anyway), a bit of creativity, to be ready to experiment – and to have plenty of high spirits. This is all you need to benefit from the numerous positive side effects of joint activities.

Special equipment, experience in training or physical fitness is not necessary. "Just play!" is the motto of the activities presented in this book. This is why you won't find any difficult exercises or tricks, but just games, at which you and your dog can go straight ahead and be successful. Be inspired to try it yourself. Have a good time discovering the unlimited possibilities of playing!

A cardboard box, a piece of food and lots of fun: many activities are that easy.

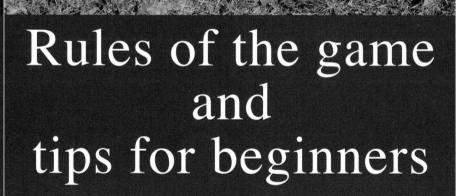

Rules of the game
and
tips for beginners

There are a few things you should look out for so that you and your dog will be able to truly enjoy these joint activities. Take your time to read through the rules of the game: your canine partner will thank you for doing so by having even more fun!

The right game

Most of the exercises described in this book should, of course, be playable for all people and all dogs. However please use common sense and think of your dog's capabilities when choosing a game.

You don't need to make a big effort to have fun: Mücke shows us how dogs in their prime can stay mentally fit.

Tiffi loves small challenges because she always gets something delicious!

Your arthritis-ridden senior will thank you for not expecting him to jump over big obstacles. This wouldn't be good for your small puppy either. An especially nervous dog doesn't have to walk across the big, threatening, rustling plastic cover straight away, or jump over the neighbours' kid's arms and legs during "people-agility" and so on. You can decide best for yourself what is good for your dog.

Dogs that enjoy easy-to-do activities in the beginning set themselves up for success at games together at a later date. Always take care that you only use equipment for your games that can't hurt or injure your dog.

Rewards are the key to success

Reward the dog for playing with you? This might seem a little strange at first: aren't you satisfying him simply by being with him? You are certainly right! Most dogs enjoy sharing activities with their humans. Many games are like little exercises, though, that the dog has to learn first. Not every dog, for instance, is successful in walking through a tunnel set up of chairs and blankets or balancing over a wall at the first go. And why should he climb up a tree trunk? Or rush up to his family with his ears flying in the wind, when playing the come game?

Now it is your turn: you have to get across to your dog how much fun this can be and how successful he can become. You, too, learn best and faster, those things that you do voluntarily and willingly and that you are really interested in. And aren't you also much more motivated when something is really worthwhile? In this regard, our dogs aren't any different from us humans. And this is why we count on rewards during joint activities. You will see your dog play along enthusiastically and dare new challenges with pleasure. You can celebrate joint success and really have fun together!

Food works best

Your dog will tell himself which reward is best for him. Most dogs don't really make an effort just for kind words, and rightly so. Stroking and touch are preferable for quality time on the sofa and usually don't go down well in training. Play or throwing a toy is more for toy junkies. But this often disturbs the activities. So food is usually the best choice. It is easy to handle and it motivates the dog.

Do you already see your dog as a four-legged sausage rolling through your apartment? Don't panic, just use a part of his normal daily ration when playing together and let him work for it a little bit. Most dogs enjoy earning their food that way!

Your basic equipment for nearly all games is food rewards. When you start a new game or work with your dog in unfamiliar situations or environments, use really attractive treats in the beginning. In everyday situations you can just use part of his normal dog food.

When you and your dog are out and about, a waist bag is ideal to store your treats.

The better you know what really makes your dog excited, the better you can reward him. Make up a list of things your dog likes best: put down his top five favourite treats. Think about things that he likes just as well as his food, for instance like running or searching or catching his ball.

Step-by-step to success

Always remember: while you already have an idea of what your dog should do, he doesn't have the slightest idea in the beginning. And you can't explain it to him either, because dogs don't understand human language.

Think about how you would feel if you were alone in a foreign country. You don't speak the national language and somebody tries to get something across to you. What would make you feel better: someone who keeps talking at you, grabs your arms and hustles you around, friendly at first but then more and more impatient because you still don't understand what is expected from you? Or a nice interpreter who would help you find your way gradually, in a calm and friendly way? The latter would, of course, be more appreciated. And your dog feels the same in our world.

It is therefore your duty to introduce your dog step-by-step to all the new challenges. Be an example of endurance and patience. Try to do so without touching, pulling or pushing your dog into the right position completely during training. Never yank his collar or lead. As long as the environment is adequate (your dog's security always comes first!), you do best in training without a leash at all.

With a treat in your hand like a magnet, you can lead your dog into any position. This alternative is suggested within the instructions of this book because this is the easiest way for most of the dog-owner-teams in the beginning. For those who like more of a challenge, you can teach your dog to follow your empty hand and give him the reward out of the other hand or a pocket. Those who are familiar with clicker training can do completely without luring the dog, and can let him figure out the exercise himself. The less you have to lure the dog, the faster your dog will understand a game.

Reaching the goal step-by-step: at first Ronja finds it quite strange to step into the box. Manuela therefore rewards her for every little improvement. Every other paw in the box is worth a treat. Success is not long in coming!

If he doesn't just follow the treat without looking, he will better realise what happens during the exercise. Of course, he still gets lots of treats.

However you proceed and whatever game you play with your dog, always take care that you keep the requirements simple in the beginning. Don't expect the perfect end result at first, but rather reward even the tiniest progress.

How this works in detail is explained within the instructions for the respective activities. All games are described so that people and dogs with no training experience can also understand them.

How to teach your dog to follow your empty hand:

• First hold a treat in your fingers and ask your dog to follow your hand. When he does so successfully, give him the treat.

• Now hide the treat in your fist so that your dog can't see it and can hardly smell it. Ask him to follow your hand again and then reward him.

• During the next step, you still reward your dog for following your hand but the treat comes from your other hand. Deliver the treats quickly out of a container or your treat bag.

• Repeat this procedure a few times until your dog gets used to it. Keep the hand that the dog is following empty but hold it as if there was food in there! Your dog will probably still follow it – and you can reward him immediately with the available food.

• Practise this regularly. Let your dog follow your empty hand for a little further each time before he is rewarded from the other hand.

Accurate timing

Even though you won't find complex exercises and tricks in this book, a little knowledge of our dogs learning behaviour might be useful. Accurate timing, for instance, is very important. Dogs learn quickest when they understand what they are rewarded for. To achieve this, you have to be as fast as lightning when rewarding them! When your dog does something that you like, you have little more than a second to react. Otherwise it is likely that your dog won't really know what he is getting his reward for.

The easiest way is to choose a short and clear word, a marker word, that you always say the moment your dog is doing something great and has earned a reward for it: try "good", "hey" or "yes" for instance. In order that your dog understands the meaning of your marker word as an announcement of a reward, say it to him a few times and immediately give him a tasty treat. After that you can use your word during play and training.

By the way, this is the principle clicker training is based on: with the aid of a clear sound (a clicker is a little plastic box with a metal tongue inside that makes a clicking sound), you can clearly indicate the behaviour required of a dog. Through accurate timing and rewarding the tiniest attempt at showing the right behaviour, the dog always knows exactly what his trainer is expecting from him. "Clicker-dogs" therefore are especially enthusiastic training partners. They work very single-handed and show a lot of own initiative.

Helpful training assistants

For some games, for instance when trying the tunnel during the living room course or the come game in the garden, it can be useful or even necessary that you await your dog with a treat at the other side or the end. If your dog has learned to wait at a certain spot, that's great. If not, then a human assistant can be of help, staying with the waiting dog. He can, for instance, use a treat to help your dog stay in position. He could also carefully hold on to the dog. This will be most comfortable for your dog when he is wearing a harness. That your helper shouldn't try to hang on to a struggling dog goes without saying.

Shared fun means doubled fun: a two legged team-mate can not only offer useful help but also enjoy playing with the dog too. You can include your whole family if you like.

Keep it simple and easy

Keep your play and training sessions short and frequent rather than long and exhausting. A few minutes at a time are more than enough in the beginning!

Always end your play with that feeling of success. If your dog does not manage the new challenge, take a step back and reward him for something he can already do.

What if it doesn't work?

There are always situations in which nothing seems to work. Then think like a good instructor: ask yourself how you could improve in order that your dog can be successful and understand you. Consider how to change the training situation so that your dog can get on with it as your own personal challenge. Lower the criteria for instance, reward him more frequently, choose an environment with fewer distractions and so on. Take into consideration that your dog also has a bad day from time to time and isn't always in optimum shape.

And when you realise that despite all efforts a game doesn't work or you and your dog aren't really having fun, then just try something different first. Problems often disappear in this way.

Stubbornness and impatience, nasty words and getting rough shouldn't be part of your joint play. Make it your aim to completely avoid saying "no", "stop it" or whatever. Try to get across to your dog what you want from him in a nice and gentle way instead of diffusing stress and bad temper!

Short and successful training sessions make you both want more! Finish playing while your dog is still concentrating and dedicated.

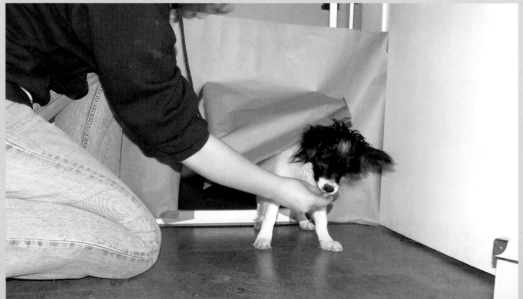

Your dog is the best indicator of good mood

Your dog will always tell you whether playing with you is really fun and relaxing for him. Become familiar with his body language and his expressions and learn to read him. Excitement, barking and jumping around or excessive panting during play, for instance, are a sign of too much agitation and that your dog probably can't cope with the situation. A tucked tail, ears back, a stiff or crouched posture can show that your dog doesn't feel comfortable at the moment.

Maybe your dog gives off so-called calming signals during some of the games, like licking his nose, blinking, yawning, turning his head away or sniffing the ground. This is your dog telling you that he feels a little uncomfortable.

Now it's your turn again. Consider changing the training situation. Little things often improve the situation such as crouching down, for instance, instead of bending over the dog, giving him a little more space or lowering your criteria and keeping the training steps smaller. In case of doubt choose a different exercise, one that your dog likes better and that makes him feel really comfortable!

CALMING SIGNALS

On the one hand, calming signals are little signs of politeness while interacting with other dogs and humans. On the other hand, they are given off frequently when dogs feel uncomfortable or when they realise that somebody else – a dog or a human – is worried. By looking out for your dog's calming signals and reacting accordingly, you offer your dog a good piece of quality of life – not only during joint play. Frequently used calming signals are:

- Licking the nose
- Blinking the eyes
- Turning of the head or the whole body
- Yawning
- Slow movements/freezing
- Sitting or lying down
- Sniffing the ground
- Play position
- Lifting up one paw
- A curving instead of a direct approach
- Splitting: one dog walks in between two other dogs or people to defuse a potential conflict from his point of view
- In some situations even peeing

Do you speak "dog"? Then you have probably realised immediately what a big challenge this apparently easy exercise is for little Fredo. It takes a lot of courage to get the treat out of the cardboard box. Always keep an eye on what your dog is telling you during training sessions. Photos: J. Hannemann

By the way, while developing this book we tried to make sure that our photo shoots were pleasant and stress-free experiences for our four-legged friends; around 40 dogs and their owners were participating. Pictures were taken mostly in people's homes or in other familiar environments, places where the dogs felt comfortable. Most dogs are demonstrating games that are already part of their daily life.

When children are participating

Many of the activities described are in the truest sense of the word child's play. Of course, it is great when the whole family is involved in playing with the dog. Child and dog can have a lot of fun together and learn a lot from each other at the same time. In the beginning, just keep an eye on children and dogs playing together and help your offspring in dealing with the dog correctly. Explain the rules of handling a dog to children and make sure that both participants feel good during joint activities.

How to manage the multi-dog household

Are you among those happy people who have the pleasure of living together with several dogs in your household? Then you can easily

Child and dog can be great playmates. With a little support, both feel great during joint activities.

include several dogs into some of the games. For instance, why not make two or three dogs climb up a tree trunk at the same time, instead of just one?

Dogs that are not food-aggressive can also enjoy searching for food together: the larger the area, and the more space they have, the better.

With many other exercises though, you will get complete chaos if several dogs hang around together. You could then do yourself and your dogs a bigger favour by practising a bit of management. If your dogs have learned to stay in one place on command, then dog 1 can wait by the side while dog 2 is playing a game with you. Dog 1 is rewarded for waiting just as well as dog 2 for the successful game. Then you continue, swapping roles.

For many dogs and people, this alternative is too stressful though, especially when waiting quietly isn't possible. In this case, dog 1 enjoys a little time out in another room. His waiting time can easily be sweetened with a chew, for instance, or a food-stuffed rubber toy. That way you kill two birds with one stone: you can enjoy a quiet training session and both dogs are usefully occupied. This is how you can also proceed if you have even more dogs living in your household!

Now we are finally ready! You are optimally primed for your joint activities now. Browse the book and choose those activities that you and your dog like best. It doesn't make any difference at which point you start and in which order you try them out. Enjoy playing together!

In order to make it really fun for dogs and people, the most important rules of the game are summarised below.

- Adapt a range of games suited to your dog's abilities.
- Only use equipment your dog can't hurt himself with.
- Treats are the perfect reward for successfully completed exercises. Use part of the daily food allowance.
- With a treat in your hand, you can lure your dog in the right direction during a lot of exercises. Those who want more, teach their dog to follow the empty hand.
- Keep the criteria low in the beginning and reward every little progress.
- The reward has to be delivered quickly in order for the dog to understand what he is rewarded for. "marker word" can be extremely helpful.
- Don't push or pull your four-legged friend. Never lose your patience and good temper.
- Keep your play sessions short. A few minutes are enough!
- Always end with a feeling of success.
- Your dog's body language tells whether he feels comfortable or if you have to change the situation.
- Keep an eye on dogs and children playing together.
- In a multi-dog household, you should play many games separately.

Whatever game you and your dog are trying out, the main thing is that you both have fun.

Sniffing games for super-noses

As we all know, our dogs are a whole lot better at smelling than we humans are. Their sense of orientation is mainly based on using the nose. Tasks in which our four-legged friends can use their olfactory organ, therefore, are especially funny for them. And there is much more to be said for nose-work: using the nose gives the dog's brain something to work on and encourages concentration. Nose-work occupies the dog without over-exciting him. It makes dogs tired without exhausting them too much. Sniffing is not only a valuable activity for hunting breeds, that have nose-work running in the blood, it is generally a guarantee for a satisfied, even-tempered dog.

Beginners' class

In the beginners', class, you can get going straight away. Hide a few treats wherever you like and let your dog search for them. That sounds easy and it really is. That's the good thing about searching for treats! It is extremely easy to do, your dog will enjoy it and it really gives him something to do. Furthermore, there are a lot of variations possible. You can hide your treats everywhere: in your own living room, as well as in the garden or on a walk, during nice or bad weather. Searching for treats is also an ideal distraction when your dog has to be home alone: you hide the food and while he is searching for it, you can leave without him worrying.

At first, rescue dog, Amore, is not used to searching for treats. A really simple search game makes him acquire a taste for it. Nose-work games are a valuable and soothing activity, especially for easily excitable dogs like Amore.

A single piece of food can occupy your dog for minutes! You can hide treats for your dog (almost) wherever you want and let him search for them.

Tips for nose-work games
• Basically searching for food is self-explanatory. The dog sees and smells the treats and goes looking for them.
• When you know that your dog is unable to sit still while you are preparing the search game, prepare ahead. Let your dog wait outside, or ask a human assistant for help, before you lose your temper and stress your dog with needless, and usually ineffective, "no" and "stop it". Your helper can distract the dog a little bit or carefully keep hold of it.
• If you like, you can announce the beginning of your search-work with a certain expression (for instance "find it"). Instruct your dog the moment he discovers there are laid out treats and wants to find them.

Such a verbal cue can be useful if you want to expand the searching activities later on and if your dog needs to search for smaller amounts of food in a wider place. In this way, you can communicate his task to him before he gets to smell the treats.

- The treats you use during search-work are, of course, taken from your dog's daily allowance. Why not plan to use part of the daily food allowance in this way?

Searching for a meal

It's so easy to liven up your dog's daily routine: instead of always feeding him from his bowl, you can scatter the food around your apartment or the garden, from time to time, and your dog can search for it. If your four legged friend eats canned or fresh food, you can hide the bowl or divide his meal into several servings and hide them in several bowls or on plates. If your dog is still untrained, make it easy for him and keep the area he has to search very small.

Where is your breakfast? Still a little bit cautiously, but with growing enthusiasm, Rover is searching for his meal in a field. Despite his handicap, he enjoys playing: Rover is blind and therefore completely reliant on his sense of smell

Hidden treats

Build a few challenges into your search-work. Choose floor coverings and surfaces the dog can't immediately spot the treats on - grained wooden floors, patterned carpets, in the grass, amongst leaves, on gravel or in the sand, for example.

Asta gets part of her meal spread out on a gravel walk. Now her nose is in great demand to find the food.

Lisa's nose gets something to do here. The treats are hidden between the towels.

Search-work in the dark

Here your super-nose can show that he is in excellent form. Arrange a few treats in a shaded room, turn out the lights and let your dog search. As soon as he knows what is going on, he will definitely find a tiny treat in a completely dark room without much of an effort. By the way, this game also works well while out for a walk on dark winter evenings. Just scatter around a few treats and let your dog search for them.

Dusty has completely entered into the box and forages busily for food in there.

Treats hidden in a pile of blankets

Crumple an old blanket or several towels on the ground. Hide the treats in the crinkles and let your sniffing champion search for them.

zling and sniffing fun begins. You can also use some old cloths or socks in your box and hide the treats in between.

The sniffing box

For this game you need a plastic or cardboard box. Make sure that you choose the right size so that your dog can easily reach over the edge with his nose and investigate its content. Screw up some newspaper and fill the box with it. Then put some treats on top and in between. The nuz-

Take a plunge

Take a look at what your dog does when you put a bit of unsinkable dry food into his water bowl, or another bowl. He will first sniff the goodies and then cleverly fish them out of the water. If your dog is splashing too much, you should move these activities outside. On a walk, you can also start searching in a puddle – in this case, your dog has to try even harder.

Searching the three dimensions

If your dog is already an experienced seeker, it's time for the third dimension. Hide your treats on a low shelf, put them on chairs, on a tree trunk outside, or hang them up on a low branch.

Queenie follows a smelling track and finds an especially delicious goody at the end. What looks like a very easy task here on the white tiles becomes a bigger challenge on grass, forest soil or a patterned carpet – and especially if the treats are only crumb sized!

Laying a scent track

Why don't you lay out a track out of tiny treat crumbs for your dog? When he follows it, he finds a great reward at the end. If you do this outside you could also pull a slice of sausage over the grass. Lead your dog to the starting point of this track and watch how he follows it – and finds the sausage at the end.

Toys instead of treats

If you have a toy maniac at home, he will search for the hidden toy with the same eagerness as his treats. In the beginning, hide the toy in an easy place while he is watching. Your dog will definitely rush forward to find the treasured object – and that way he will get an idea of what is going on

Asta was not at all prepared for that: she immediately smelled the treat. She first thoroughly scans the ground, before she begins to look. The smells come from above, the treat is hung up in the bushes!

here. Later on ask your dog to wait where he can't see where you are hiding his toy.

The disadvantage of searching for toys is that treats can be consumed on the spot while toys have to be given back. Teams that haven't practised this yet could get into trouble. But if throwing balls and sticks is part of your daily life anyway then start by hiding the toy from time to time instead of throwing it. While chasing flying balls and sticks frequently excites the dog, search-work encourages calmness and concentration.

You want even more?

Heighten the criteria for all of your search games step-by-step:

- When searching for treats, reduce the number of treats scattered around.
- If your dog is an enthusiastic toy seeker, make the hiding place increasingly difficult to find.
- You can also pretend to be hiding toys or treats, bending down obviously in different places, while your dog is watching. In this way, your dog doesn't see exactly where you are actually placing the object.
- Enlarge your search area gradually. When your dog knows the games and has a little bit of practice, he will rummage through your entire living room, parts of your garden or a large box for just one treat without much of an effort.

Maike is a toy fan. She is always ready to play hide and seek with her favourite toy. While Maike is waiting around the corner, Silke hides the ball under the rug. No problem! Maike's good nose shows her the way to the toy quickly!

Coda has become a real search pro. He has no idea where in this big field his toy is hidden. It is fascinating to watch how he searches the whole area in wide circles fast as lightning … and finds the desired object within a short time!

Scent discrimination the easy way

It's child's play for dogs to discriminate one scent from another or to detect certain scents. We can integrate this into our everyday play.

The shell game

The objective of this game is for your dog to use his nose and show you where the treat is hidden.

You will need

- Several colanders or, alternatively, over turned flower pots, that have holes at the bottom through which your dog can smell the treats.
- And lots of treats.

This is how it works:

- Place the colanders on the ground one after the other.
- While your dog is awaiting his mission, you lift all the colanders quickly and hide some treats under just one of them.
- Observe what your dog is doing. You can definitely spot under which one of them he finds the treats through his reactions while sniffing the colanders. Maybe he scratches the chosen one with his paw, maybe his tail starts wagging excitedly, or he tries to get his muzzle under the colander.
- Reward this behaviour immediately by lifting up the colander and letting him have the treats.
- Next time, put the treats under one of the other colanders.

Weimaraner, Beppo, is waiting curiously. One colander after another is lifted but the treats are only hidden underneath one of them! As a nose-work expert, Beppo finds the right colander immediately – and gets his reward.

Sniffing for professionals

Would you like to get into scent discrimination a little deeper? You can teach your dog quite easily to choose the only object that has the smell of his owner on it out of several similar ones. You think this is difficult? For your dog, this game is as easy as telling the difference between a red and a green spot is for you.

You have probably already tried the easiest version of scent discrimination unconsciously. Have you been throwing sticks or a pinecone for your dog from time to time? (Caution: sticks or parts of them can bore into the dog's throat and injure him severely!) I'm sure you have done this on a walk when lots of sticks and pinecones are lying on the ground. You don't need to be a visionary to be quite sure that your dog, despite all the other similar objects around him, has brought back to you the one you have thrown. You see, your dog is a born scent discrimination expert.

If your dog likes to play fetch and if you would like to get to the bottom of this phenomenon, you can try out the following:

- First you and your dog play a little with a certain pinecone. That way your dog gets interested in it and it absorbs the smell.
- While you are playing, place the cone close to several other cones.
- Does your dog pick up the right cone and bring it back to you? He probably will!

For your equipment you will need several similar objects (for instance beer mats, rags, or pine cones), a barbecue prong or an unused disposable glove, as well as tasty treats. Only touch the object your dog will be looking for later on. All other objects are to be touched with the prong or the glove.

For several minutes, take the object your dog is to search for later in your hand or put it in your pocket. This way it will absorb your smell.

Your dog has probably already done this. You are playing with a pinecone, throwing or laying it next to others – and he brings this special cone back to you. Try it out. Every dog is a scent discrimination expert!

Show the smelly object to your dog. Play with it together for a while. If your dog is not an enthusiastic player, reward him for any interest he shows in the object with a marker word (or a clicker, in case your dog knows it) and immediately follow with a treat.

You can systematically train this sort of nose-work not only if your dog is not so much into playing fetch but also when you want to expand your scent discrimination activities to all kinds of objects. Take a look at the following picture series to see how it works.

Put the object on the ground or throw it away a bit. Your dog will probably run after it immediately. Reward any reaction that shows that the dog has perceived the object, whether he is sniffing it, nudging it, taking it into his mouth or just sitting in front of it and looking at you. After a few tries, you can start giving your dog a verbal cue (for instance "find it" or "find mine") to send him to the object.

Now you add a second neutrally smelling object. Place it on the ground by using the prongs or the gloves. Place the object with your smell on it next to it at a small distance. Your dog will now take a look at those objects.

Reward your dog immediately for any reaction to the correct object – even if it seems to be accidentally in the beginning! If your dog takes a neutral object into his mouth by mistake, or if you touch it, don't reward him, but replace it and have another try.

Observe your dog carefully while he is sniffing the objects. He will probably tell you with a special announcement behaviour when he has found the correct object. He might be sniffing more intensely, wagging his tail quickly, looking at you, nudging the object or picking it up. Reward him for doing so! Practise several times and change the position of the objects in between. Make sure that you don't put the neutral objects on the same spot where the correct object was placed before. Relocating the training area a few metre away after every session works best.

Step-by-step, add more and more neutrally smelling objects. Later on you can also ask other people to touch the neutral objects so that your dog has to discriminate between several different humans' smells. Maybe you would like to play shoe- or sock-memory where your dog has to distinguish your socks or shoes from other family members' or visitors' shoes or socks?

Quick introduction to tracking

People find it especially fascinating to watch dogs following a track. Maybe you have the image of a police dog following a suspect's track in your mind now. Don't let your thoughts wander too far - your dog is an expert in tracking, too! Think about how often he suddenly uses his nose during walks and is obviously following a track - a rabbit's, neighbour's cat's, a friend's or his favourite person's track.

We humans are not really able to teach our dogs anything about tracking with our restricted sense of smell. But we can make it a big pleasure for them when we join in making an excursion into the world of smells. Integrate your dog's natural pre disposition into your games!

Start with a little experiment on your walk:

Every dog is an expert in searching for tracks – so is yours!

- Ideally you should have a family member or good friend with you (one your dog likes very much). Your dog should be wearing a harness and walking on a quite long lead (experts are using a ten metre tracking leash). Your helper has some tasty treats with him.
- Somewhere along your way you make a stop. Your helper goes ahead a few steps taking the treats with him while your dog looks on. After about 30 steps, your helper leaves the path to left or right and hides in the bushes or around a corner and waits there. Your dog shouldn't be able to see him anymore then.
- Your dog will, of course, be waiting impatiently to follow his two-legged friend. He wants to retrieve him! Keep the lead long, follow your dog and observe what he is doing. He will be using all his senses to find your helper.
- When your dog has reached his destination have a party! Be happy about his success and be very generous with treats.

Your dog's well-developed nose helps find his friend quickly. For a dog, this is the most natural thing in the world, for us humans, it is fascinating every time.

When they are searching for something, dogs first use their eyes, then they smell with their nose high up in the air and, as a last possibility, they sniff the ground.

It will, of course, happen from time to time that your dog doesn't reach his destination. This has nothing to do with him not being able to smell well enough or to follow a track. In the beginning, in most cases, our dogs are just not used to searching for a track together with us. The wind also blows unfavourably sometimes and carries the scent away. That's no problem. Just have another go straight away for a shorter distance and fast success! Never be impatient and don't reprimand your dog.

Searching for tracks with a hunting dog: doesn't this stimulate the hunting instinct all the more?

Your dog knows how to follow a track anyway! As you are only following human tracks your dog learns that there are other interesting things to do in the forest than to rouse all kinds of game. Tracking satisfies the natural needs of your dog and is an ideal substitution for hunting!

Don't be astonished if your dog does not constantly keep his nose sticking to the ground, if he is not walking exactly on your helper's track, or is taking a short cut, this is because the scents are blown away by the wind and are sometimes situated next to the track.

Have you and your dog got hooked on this? Then your helper may walk a farther distance and include one or two corners. Of course, you adjust the difficulty to your dog's abilities. The picture series shows you how you can even make your dog follow a track when there is no helper waiting at the end.

Your dog (dressed up for work with a harness and a 10-metre leash) accompanies you and your helper to a starting point in a field or in the forest. Your helper has a plastic bag or container filled with treats and tied to a rope and he lets your dog sniff it.

Keep the lead slack and follow your dog. He will now use all his senses to find the hidden treats. He looks around, smells in the air and sniffs the ground.

While your dog is watching, the helper starts walking. He marks the beginning of the track with an object that carries his scent on it (for instance a piece of cloth or a jacket). To make the track really interesting for the dog, your helper lets the treat container or bag drag over the ground behind him for the first ten steps.

Let your dog work on his own, don't say anything and don't correct him. If he is completely wrong, just stand still and see if he finds his way back onto the right track himself. If not, give him a new chance on a new track. Tracking is result orientated; depending on how the wind is blowing, it is likely that your dog is walking next to the track or is taking a short cut. In the picture, the dog is walking straight up to the treat box.

Your helper then walks in an L-shape: after 30 steps straight ahead, he then makes a turn to the left or to the right. After about another 30 steps, he puts the treat box to the ground (hidden behind some grass or a log, so that it is not visible immediately), walks on for a few metres in the same direction and returns to the starting point in a wide curve. There the dog is waiting and is hopefully highly motivated to find the treats.

When you reach the destination have a big party. Open the treat box and feed your dog from it. Change harness or lead to show your dog that he has completed the task. If you want to lay some more tracks, make sure to use an area where neither you nor the helper have left a trace. You can easily go tracking in different environments, with different people and for different lengths of track. By the way, you can also lay the track for your dog yourself.

Willingness is capitalised upon when doing living room agility! Those who succeed without pushing or pulling the dog, are rewarded with an enthusiastic four-legged teammate prepared to approach new challenges more and more fearlessly in the future.

Living room agility

So, the weather is really bad again, it's getting dark earlier, but you still want to pep up yourself and your dog a little? Then turn your living room into an adventure playground temporarily! Don't worry; you don't have to rearrange your house. Just use those things that are available anyway and set up a little course with them. All kinds of exercises for dexterity and mobility are not only fun but, as little tests of courage, they also train your dog's body awareness and build up his self confidence. You become good at guiding him into all kinds of positions and in showing him the way yourself.

Tips for living room agility
- The bigger your apartment and the smaller your dog, the more space and freedom of movement you are going to have. Nevertheless, even big dogs in small apartments don't have to be neglected. Pick out those games that fit you!
- Rapid runs and big jumps are usually not possible in an apartment. On slippery floors (for instance tiles or wooden floors), you would do better without those, so that your dog doesn't get hurt when landing. Approach things comfortably and at your own pace.
- As always, when you are training your dog, don't be stingy with treats. Reward your dog for even the slightest success and not just for the desired end product. Celebrate every managed step.
- Remember: to get the dog into the desired position, don't touch him but rather use your treat hand as a magnet. If your dog is used to the clicker you can let him figure out all the exercises himself through free shaping.
- When you are introducing new objects, let your dog sniff them thoroughly first to get used to them.
- Keep an eye on how your dog is feeling towards your inventive fantasy obstacles. Does he show signs of discomfort? Then make it easier for him, reward him more often or change to another exercise.

Various fantasy obstacles

You definitely have certain things in your household that you can perfectly integrate into your games. For your personal living room agility course you hardly need any equipment that you don't already have anyway.

The 'curtain'
Tie a rope between two backrests or tie up a broomstick to the backrests (see photograph). Now you have the basic equipment for all kinds of tests of courage.

What your 'curtain' is made of is up to you.
Photo: A. Lüke

For instance, you can tie any of the following to the rope or the broomstick
- cloths
- paper strips
- threaded beer mats or cardboard rolls.

Can you make your dog walk through this 'curtain'?

This is how it works very easily:
- First your dog should be able to brush aside the curtain without much of an effort. Therefore start with few, light items.
- Now let your dog pick up some treats from the ground around the curtain or reward him for just touching the curtain lightly.
- If you are ready, waiting for your dog on the other side, it is easier for your dog to walk through the curtain. If you are agile and flexible you can even crawl ahead in the beginning!

What a test of courage for little Leeroy. To make it easy for him in the beginning, two buckets help keep the flap up. Later on, Leeroy has to push a little harder, until he finally opens the flap all alone.

The dog flap

Stick a piece of wrapping paper to a door-frame and cut a dog flap into it. Motivate your dog to walk through the flap.
- Waiting for your dog on the other side with a treat in your hand works best.
- Help your dog by lifting the flap up a little if he doesn't dare do it himself in the beginning.
- If your dog is very scared, you can cut the flap into strips or let him walk through a little hole without a flap at first.

Weave poles and mobility games

As you can imagine, chair or table-legs make perfect weave pole elements. But there are many more things your dog can weave through:
- You can for instance lead him through a plastic bottle slalom.
- Indoor plants on plant-rollers can also be circled excellently.
- Advanced mobility experts hold a closed umbrella or a broomstick upright, with point to the ground, in one hand and make their dog circle it with the aid of the other hand.

Indoor plants on plant-rollers can be circled.
Photo: A. Luke

A light blanket, a piece of tape and a doorframe – there you have a
living room hurdle. Zito shows us how it works. Photo: A. Luke

This is how it works especially well:

- If your dog is still untrained, don't expect a perfect slalom but reward him for following your hand just a little bit. Keep the number of the poles low.

Living room obstacles for high achievers

Depending on the size of the apartment and the dog as well as the flooring, you can include jumps in your living room agility. Appropriately low jumping elements can be built out of different items such as:

- rolled up blankets
- narrow shelves
- empty plastic flower boxes, or
- retained broomsticks

This is how your dog learns to jump:

- Make it easy for him in the beginning. Arrange your obstacle so that your dog ideally can't pass beside or underneath it. Use doorframes or chairs as lateral restrictions.

- Encourage your dog to jump over the hurdle with the aid of some treats. You can jump together with him in the beginning. Or you step over the hurdle first, and then lure your dog over to the other side.

- When your dog has understood the game and has tried different obstacles, you can insert a verbal cue (for instance the word "jump") and send your dog over the hurdle with it.

Never-ending tunnels and tubes

Tunnels enjoy great popularity as tests of courage during living room agility. You can for instance:

- set up an open tunnel with several chairs in a row
- place a blanket over a (coffee) table

- make a tube out of a rolled camping mat with a piece of tape
- divert your children's play tunnel from its intended use
- make a tunnel out of a large cardboard box

The shorter and wider the tunnel is, the easier it is for your dog to start! If possible, pen in the tunnel between chair or table-legs or a door frame so that it doesn't roll away or turn over.

This is how you pitch the tunnel to your dog:

- Throw a few treats that your dog can pick up into the beginning of the tunnel.
- Position yourself at the other end of the tunnel and hand your dog rewards through the tunnel.
- The more cautious your dog is, the more generously you reward the tiniest steps. Your dog doesn't have to go through the whole tunnel at once. Share his happiness when he dares to stick his head through for a moment.
- Most importantly, for this exercise, never push or pull your dog into the tunnel!

Meggan masters the camping mat tunnel with flying colours.

The collapsed tunnel adventure

This is the tunnel for the advanced dog: the tunnel ends in a form of open-ended sack and your dog has to push himself out at the other end.

- You need a chair (alternatively a coffee table) and a blanket.
- Place the blanket over the chair so that it hangs down two opposite sides – like with a normal tunnel. Unlike the normal tunnel, there should be a lot of overhang at the end so that the blanket behind the chair lies on the floor, as a sort of sack.
- Very important: the blanket has to be attached to the chair so that it can't slip off while your dog is walking through it! Such an accident could totally spoil your dog's fun with the tunnel.

And this is how it works:

- Your dog is waiting in front of the tunnel. If he hasn't learned to wait yet, then ask a human assistant to stay with him and to keep hold of him, carefully if necessary.
- You go to the other end of the tunnel. Pick up the end that is lying on the floor and catch your dog's eye. Call him and reward him, when he comes to you through the (open) tunnel.
- During the next few steps, lower the opening of the tunnel gradually so that your dog gets a feeling of pushing himself through to the exit.
- By the way: keep the degree of difficulty low in the beginning with the tunnel

Step-by-step, Asta's coffee table tunnel turns into a test of courage.

sack rather short. Your dog only has to walk a short distance in the dark then.

Hoops and other openings

For this game you need a big enough hula hoop. Your dog ought to be able to jump or walk through it now.

- This works especially well in the beginning when you have your hands free. Ask an assistant to keep hold off the hoop. Alternatively pen in the hoop between two chairs to the left and to the right. At this stage of the game the hoop is still touching the ground.
- Lure your dog through the hoop.
- If he is walking through it happily and confidently, again and again, you can keep hold of the hoop yourself. When your dog is situated on the right side of the hoop, then take it into your right hand and a treat into your left hand and lure him through the hoop from the right side to the left side with your treat. When your dog is situated on the left side of the hoop, then take the hoop into your left hand and your treat into the right hand.
- Gradually hold the hoop a little higher so that your dog has to jump or - if your dog is bigger - has to step through. Keep in mind that most apartments don't offer enough space for big jumps!

Would you like to try some variations?
- Stick a piece of wrapping paper between

Together you can have even more fun when dog and owner step through a big hoop together.

rustling plastic covers. So why not try a little test of courage in a familiar environment? You can integrate these into your course:

- plastic bags and plastic covers
- doormats made of different fibres
- newspaper (unfolded or rumpled and placed into a shallow cardboard box)
- aluminium foil
- non-slip mats for bathtubs or showers
- an air mattress with only a little air in it (provided that your dog doesn't have too sharp claws)
- a bookshelf

Let your dog investigate the unknown surfaces step-by-step on his own. Every little test of courage passed – even if it is only placing one paw on the different surfaces in the beginning – is worth a reward and gives your dog a little bit of self-confidence which carries into his everyday life.

Sun walks across a plastic cover. With a little bit of practice, every dog eventually approaches all kinds of surfaces with more and more self-confidence.

the door frames, cut a big circle-shaped opening into it and let your dog jump through it.

- If your hoop is big enough, you can do step through the hoop together with him.

Challenges on the ground

You probably have already observed that your dog avoids passing grids or doesn't like

Co-ordination exercises with a ladder

Most dogs have problems using their hind legs consciously. With your living room agility games, you can combine fun and co-ordination exercises by using your household ladder!

- Lay the ladder on the ground and slowly lead the dog over it. It doesn't matter if he places his paws on or in between the ladder steps.
- If your dog has problems with this task, praise and reward him for every little step initially.
- You can also throw some treats between the ladder steps for your dog. While searching, he may walk over the ladder independently.
- Those who don't have a ladder can also do the co-ordination exercises with sticks lying on the ground in the shape of a ladder or a fan, or with several hula-hoops lying on top of, and next to, each other.

Zito walks across the ladder and thereby training his co-ordination and body awareness at the same time. Photo: A. Lüke

Balancing on a wobble board

With the aid of a non-slip board, you can train your dog's balance and body awareness.

"Hey, what's that?" Leeroy is a bit suspicious about the wobble board at first. He carefully comes closer and is rewarded by Ilona for the first contact with the board. Motivated, Leeroy becomes braver. He steps onto the board, makes it move from one side to the other with his front paws, and finally steps onto it completely. Every step is worth a treat!

Mental exercise –
Challenges for bright young sparks

In this chapter, the grey matter is pepped up. You can make your dog become a smart problem solver, too. He who wants to get the treat has to think things through, use muzzle or paws, by pulling or pushing.

Mental acrobatics don't only make the dog more tired than an extensive walk – the successful solving of mental exercises builds up a dog's self-confidence and helps him

cope with everyday life. The dog that practises solving problems through playful independent thinking is able to keep his cool when it's really necessary and isn't overwhelmed by his emotions so easily.

With many of the games, you will experience how learning takes place! Observe how your dog develops strategies to achieve his goal and becomes more and more experienced in solving mental exercises, without you having to actually teach him anything.

Tips for mental exercises
- Besides rugged treat balls and harmless cardboard boxes, during mental exercises do not leave your dog to fend for himself. Always stay near him and keep an eye on your four-legged friend.
- Make sure that the objects you are using don't have any sharp edges or contain materials that could hurt your dog while he is finding out about the right strategy.
- Most of the equipment needed for mental exercises can be found in your household. If you don't yet know how your dog will be handling the objects, and if he is inexperienced in mental acrobatics, only use items you could manage without if necessary. That would be better than having to scold him if he begins work a little clumsily at first and spoils something.
- Never mind what game you are playing, your dog should be successful right from the beginning – and not after having to try hard and get frustrated. Therefore keep it very easy for him in the beginning. Help him when he doesn't get on with a problem. When your dog has understood the principle, you can increase the degree of difficulty bit by bit.

Exercises for package artists

The time when all kinds of cardboard and packaging ended up as waste paper is over, because they offer perfect mental challenges.

Fascinating cardboard boxes

Have you thought about how many different types of cardboard boxes exist? There are shoe cartons with removable and hinged lids, there are collapsible boxes, parcels in all kinds of sizes, small boxes for teabags, large packing cases, pizza cartons and so on. Any kind of cardboard box can become a challenge for your dog! Place one or several treats inside, close the lid and watch which strategy your dog develops to get inside.

Tip
Don't close the box completely at first: that makes it easier for your dog to work out the opening mechanism.

Cardboard box mountain

Does your dog already have a little experience with cardboard boxes and do you have a whole lot of empty boxes left over from an extensive shopping trip? Then why don't you surprise your dog with a whole mountain of cardboard boxes? He will have to develop a different strategy for nearly every one of those boxes to get to the tasty treats on the inside. Your dog will possibly set to work a little brutally at first. In which case,

don't scold him but be happy that you don't have to reduce them to small pieces before putting them into the dustbin. Soon your dog will discover how he can get to the treats fast as lightning in an elegant and effective way.

> **Tip**
> Especially when using narrow and long boxes (like cornflakes or cereal boxes) make sure that your dog doesn't get trapped with his head inside and become scared.

Box in a box

Here's a variation for experienced box openers: put an extremely good smelling treat inside a little box, close it and put it inside a larger box. Then close the larger box and put it inside an even bigger box and so on. Your dog now has to work his way through several

Meggan watches Marianne putting some food into a shoe carton and closing it afterwards. She uses her paw and her muzzle to open the box – and succeeds!

A different strategy for every box: Lara works her way through different packages – each one of them contains a treat for her.

A box in a box – there is a lot to be done here.

packages with different opening mechanisms to get to his destination. If your dog is not an experienced box opener yet, place a treat in every single layer – that will keep him going.

Special packages

When you walk through the shops, keep your eyes open from now on and you will see that there are packages that are real treat machines – without you having to do any handiwork. Some of them contain small drawers to pull out or cases to open and you can include them successfully in your mental exercises.

> Whatever packaging you are using, before your dog plays with them make sure that there are no remnants of the original content that could do him harm!

Here a box that contained dishwasher tablets (cleaned thoroughly) becomes a doggy gaming machine. First put a treat into the wide open case and let your dog eat out of it. Step-by-step, close the case a little more and your dog will start using his muzzle or paw to get to the sought-after treats.

Meggan shows us how the end result can look. She is very clever and even opens the smallest, firmly closed boxes.

- When your dog has understood the principle (push the lid aside to get to the treats), close the lid but leave a little gap open for your dog on one side. This way he can open the lid with his muzzle or a paw.
- When he has mastered this, close the lid completely. To make it easy for your dog, hold on tight to the box.

Instead of a treat you can also put your dog's favourite toy inside the package.

What's next?

You will suddenly find a lot of boxes that your dog could open to search for treats or toys inside - small buckets or bins, miscellaneous cartons and cases. Let your dog solve the puzzles – and in the future thoroughly protect dustbins and lunchboxes in your household that your dog shouldn't open!

How do I get to the toy? Zito has figured it out and has pushed a blanket aside to get to the desired contents of the box. Photo: A. Lüke

Tupperware party for our four-legged friends
When your dog is quite experienced in opening packages, he will probably also manage to take off the lid of a lunchbox if there is a treat inside:

- At first only put the lid loosely on top of the box. Your dog then has to push it aside to get to the content.

Maike is very clever: after a short trial and error, she pushes her nose under the edge of the bowl, flips it over – and in that way, gets to the treat lying underneath.

Just staggering

Open your kitchen units and take a look into your pantry. There is a lot of equipment for your games hidden in there.

Treats under bowls

Lay an ordinary household bowl upside down on the ground. Place a treat underneath while your dog looks on and then watch what your four-legged friend does next.

Does he cleverly push the bowl into one corner and flip it over with his nose? Does he step onto the edge with his paws and get his nose under it that way? Try this game on different surfaces - on slippery floors, on a carpet or outside on the lawn.

Flower pot challenge

Lay a big plastic flower pot upside down on the floor. Allow your dog to watch while you hide a few treats underneath, ideally

Treats under the flower pot roller board

Place a few treats under a flower pot roller board (of course without a flower on it!) What does your dog do? Initially, he will definitely, unintentionally, move the board to the side a bit while sniffing the treat – and will soon realise exactly what to do to be successful.

Felix notices exactly how the treats are put into the flower pot from above. But how can he reach the food now? The clever terrier quickly finds the solution. For rescue dogs like him, mental exercises like these are a welcome enrichment of their daily life.

Their ongoing appetite turns Beagles into motivated mental workers. Fredo is working successfully on the roller board. Photo: K. Schomburg

by dropping them through the holes in the bottom of the pot. Your dog will immediately locate the tempting smells with his nose – but he can't reach them directly!

Does he step onto the edge with his paws and get his nose under it that way? Try this game on different surfaces - on slippery floors, on a carpet or outside on the lawn.

> **Tip**
>
> If your roller board has a slatted surface rather than a solid one, make sure that your dog doesn't get his paw stuck.

A game of chance under cups

Take a few sturdy yoghurt pots or plastic cups. Turn them upside down and put a treat under each one of them. Your dog now has to knock the cups over or pick them up to get to the treats. When you have

Nemo quickly finds out what he has to do here. He knocks over the potato chips box and searches for the treats that have fallen out on the ground.

Where is the treat? There is only one thing for it – turn them over and have a look. Photo: A. Lüke

played the game a few times, leave out the food under some of the cups. Now your dog has to knock over several cups before he discovers a treat.

Treat bowling

Arrange a few solid, empty potato chips boxes or similar cookie packages, without their lids, on the ground. Place a few easy rolling treats into each one of the boxes. Now it's your dog's turn, if he doesn't have a good nose, he has no chance to get to the treats. They only fall out when the boxes are knocked over. How long does it take before the accidental overturning of a box becomes your dog's intended tactic for solving this problem?

> **Tip**
>
> Do you have a dog that is sensitive to sound? To make sure that he doesn't get a fright when the boxes are knocked over, play treat bowling on a carpet or a blanket with him first.

Think outside the box

The treat is hidden under the cupboard. No chance of reaching it with the muzzle. This small beagle tries to use his paws – and succeeds! Photos: J. Hannemann

This makes your dog's head spin, now he has to puzzle quite a bit to get to his treats.

Skilful paws

Is there a bookshelf, a cupboard or a sofa in your apartment with legs just long enough to create a narrow gap to the ground? Your dog's head and body shouldn't fit into this gap but his paws should. Then enjoy another challenge of mental exercise. Put a treat under the shelf while your dog is watching and see what he does. He will soon realise that he can't use his muzzle. Will he try to fish for it with his paws?

> **Tip**
>
> Always make sure that nothing can fall down and scare your dog or even hurt him when he is in action. If there is no suitable piece of furniture in your household, just use a shelf. Lay it down on the floor and put one or two books under each end so that you get an adequate gap.

A fishing rod for your dog

This is a real experiment for problem solvers.

- Attach a piece of cord or a rope to a sought after goody, for instance a piece of dried food or a chew.
- Then slide the goody under a piece of furniture with a gap small enough that the dog can't get his head into it.
- The end of the rope sticks out clearly visible. What will your dog do? Does he pull it out with his muzzle or does he fish for it with his paws and get to his treat that way?
- Make it easy for your dog at first and position the treat so that your dog can't reach it directly but only has to pull the rope a little bit to get it out.

Don't be disappointed if your little experiment doesn't succeed at first go. First let your dog brood about some easier mental exercises and get back to this one again later on.

> **Tip**
>
> What should never happen, of course, is that in the heat of the moment your dog eats the cord attached to the treat, too. In case of doubt, use a thicker rope or put the treat into a container (for instance a small lunchbox) and attach the cord to the container.

The treat box

Owner and dog are sitting in front of a large cardboard box with the opening turned upside down. The box is also open at the back

Don't give up hope if your four-legged friend doesn't find the solution as fast as Desmond does. He is a mental exercise expert and comes up with an idea quickly pulling out the treat attached to the cord from under the cupboard in an instant. Photos: K. Schomburg

(cut a hole into it or turn down one side). All other sides are closed. Owner and dog are sitting at the front. Lift up the box a little and place an attractive treat underneath while your dog is watching. Now hold on to the box slightly, so that your dog can't lift it or knock it over. How long does it take until the dog decides to take the opening at the back instead of scratching at the closed end of the box?

Punch and Judy show

For this variation of mental exercise you also need a large cardboard box. Your dog ideally shouldn't be able to look over it.

So close and yet so unreachable, he who wants to get the treat has to literally think outside the box!

Mental exercises with a box, only he who thinks it through gets to the treat.

- This time arrange the box with the opening backwards.
- Now cut a slot into the bottom of the box, which is now at the front, that is so narrow that the dog can look through but not put his head through.
- You can play this game in two different ways, you are either behind the box and your dog is waiting in front or you are both in front.

- Place a treat in the box that is clearly visible through the slot.
- Hold on tight to the box now so that it can't be knocked over and give free rein to your dog.

What will your dog do? He can't get through the slot. How long does it take until he realises that the route to the treat leads around the box? If your dog should literally try to bang his head against the carton wall, take it easy – it is the direct route to the goal!

This mental exercise will be well received by your dog. You only need a plastic bottle, a stick and some treats.

Intelligent machines

With little effort you can construct funny gambling machines for your dog that stimulate his grey matter. Handlers with great handicraft skills can make more out of these game variations and run riot with the professional variations. There is no limit to creativity.

Spin the bottle

Spinning the bottle is one of the dog's most favourite games. You need
- a solid plastic bottle
- and a stick (for instance a bamboo pole).

And this it how it works:
- Drill two holes midway on both sides of the plastic bottle (ideally carefully with a drill) and push the stick through.
- Put in some treats, hold on to both ends of the stick, and let your dog have a go. Some

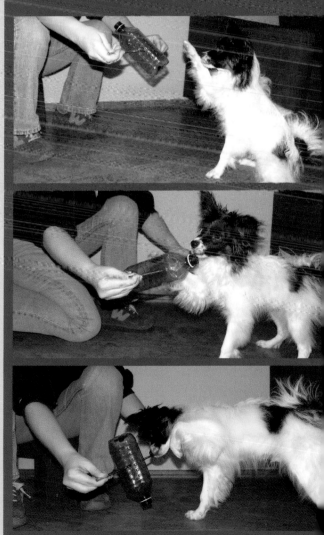

Leeroy in action: The small Papillon knows exactly how to get to the treat.

Spinning the bottle for professionals: With a few handicraft skills and a lot of imagination, the easiest basic idea can be turned into clever gambling machines. Ronnie shows us two different types. Photo: S. Putz

If you enjoy this little game, you might like the following variations:

- You can adjust the degree of difficulty of your treat machine by changing the position of the holes in the bottle. The further up the holes are situated, the harder it gets to make the bottle topple.
- If you drill several pairs of holes above each other, you can arrange different degrees of difficulty in one bottle.
- Vary the size of the bottles and see how your dog gets along with that.
- With a little effort and handicraft skills, you can build a whole bottle machine. Several bottles can be attached to one sturdy frame for your four-legged friend to let off steam with.

dogs are somehow creative enough to start to move the bottle immediately. Others can be helpless facing this challenge at first.

- As usual, make it easy for your dog and arrange for quick success. You can, for instance, turn the bottle so that even the slightest sniff, or a little touch with the dog's nose, will make the bottle topple. Only use treats that roll easily and fall out directly when the bottle is turned.

The drawer

This is how you prepare this mental challenge:

- Provide an empty cookie box from which the inner part is pulled out of the package like a drawer.
- Attach a strap to the end of this drawer. This can be a piece of tape (the sticky sides on top of each other so that the dog's nose doesn't stick to it later on) or you can drill a hole into the drawer and attach a piece of cord to it.

Your dog's job now is to pull the drawer out of the package using the strap to get to the treats inside.

- Sit in front of your dog and place a treat right in the front of the drawer.
- Those who have a clicker-trained dog won't have a problem in closing the drawer directly and in teaching the dog step-by-step to take the strap into his mouth and pull it.
- If your dog is not clicker trained, don't close the drawer completely at first but leave a little gap open. The dog's nose should just fit in there.
- Offer the cookie box to your dog at nose level.
- Now it's your dogs turn. He will definitely sniff the treats thoroughly and open the drawer by sticking his nose into it.
- When your dog has understood the principle of sticking his nose in, in order to open the drawer, you reduce the gap, bit by bit. When his nose doesn't fit into the gap anymore, your dog will probably use his teeth to pull out the drawer.
- You have nearly reached the goal. The smaller the gap gets, the more likely it is that your dog will realise that the strap is a good point to grab with his teeth. When you finally close the drawer completely, he will probably try to pull the strap.
- If your dog carefully twitches the strap rather nervously at first, help him a little bit and reward him immediately for this step in the right direction - just push out the drawer from the back and open it that way for your dog.

With only a few attempts, Maike has found out how to open the drawer. Here she shows us the perfect end result.

This time Asta has to pull out two straps to make the treat fall out.

A bit more solid, this down-pipe variation is made out of a potato chips box.

Of course your constructions made out of toilet roll or kitchen paper cardboard tube are not long lasting. They are naturally fragile and wear easily. So don't scold your dog if some of the down-pipes fall victim to his over-eagerness.

It is possible that when you and your dog are trying out several straps on top of each other, your toilet roll or kitchen paper cardboard tube construction will become too unsteady. Potato chips boxes or other solid cardboard rolls are of valuable use and can be handled almost without handicraft skills.

Are you and your dog enjoying those tube constructions? Are you technically skilled and do you have a well-equipped workshop

Turning from a cardboard roll to a gambling machine, this down-pipe is destined for more and Ronnie is happy about it! Photo: S. Putz

The height of creativity: Hovawart Dex presents us a sausage machine that leaves nothing to be desired. Photo: R. Eysel

Sitting in front of the pipe

Do-it-yourself stores are a dog-game fan's paradise. Sewage pipes, for instance, can be stuck together and turned into adventurous and mysterious combinations. How large

in your cellar? Then you might like some professional variations on these mental exercises.

You can make the most adventurous gadgets out of plastic tubes, Plexiglas tubes and wood.

Tip
The youngest two-legged family members also enjoy different kinds of tube constructions! As long as your dog is not looking out for disappearing treats or balls, you can convert your tubes into sand or water pipelines in your garden.

"What is this?" Meggan is really surprised. The treat has disappeared! Meggan literally sits in front of the tube. Only after analyzing the opening thoroughly does she walk around the tube – and find the fallen treat! After a few goes, Meggan has figured it out. She stays at the end of the tube ready to catch the treats.

and winding your construction is, and whether you can let treats or your dog's ball disappear inside and reappear elsewhere, right in front of your dog's surprised gaze, is up to you and your dog's creativity.

Faye shows us what else is doable with such a tube construction. She throws a ball into it herself and waits tensely until it comes out at the other end.

Treat balls and other food dispensers

Treat balls, food cubes and the like are some of the best items of occupational equipment, with little expenditure of time and lots of fun for your dog. The principle is always the same. You put in a measure of dried food. Your dog's job now is to move the food dispenser so that the treats fall out.

By the way, this is not the only challenge that your dog is mastering in this way. Especially when he is working on patterned floors or in your garden, his nose will be working at full speed when pushing the ball around. He doesn't want to miss a treat falling out, after all. Many dogs also quickly develop clever tactics in order to manage balls and cubes so that they don't get caught in the corners of rooms or under the furniture.

Tiffi puzzles over a treat ball.

> **Tip**
> Do you usually feed dried food? Your dog will be thrilled when you serve him his meal in a treat ball or food cube in the future instead of in his food bowl. Dogs that are fed canned food, self-cooked meals or a raw diet enjoy self-baked treats in their food dispensers.

Treat balls and food cubes are also a good way of passing the time when your dog has to stay at home alone. Try out how your dog handles the food dispenser several times while you are there and only use the especially sturdy and solid models when leaving him alone.

> Wide openings and a relatively large amount of treats make it easier for your dog in the beginning. When even the first sniff makes the food fall out, your dog will try anything to get some more.

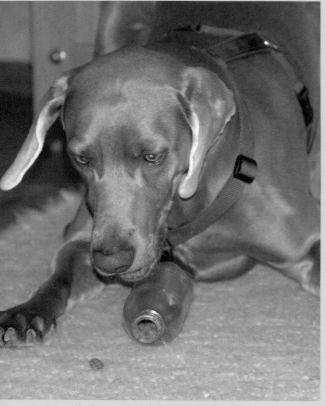

An inexpensive pleasure: Beppo is enjoying himself with a food bottle.

A solid cardboard tube with a few holes turns into an exiting food dispenser.

The food bottle

Put a bit of food into an empty plastic bottle and lay it down on the ground. Your hungry dog will now push, roll and maybe even throw around the bottle to get to the treats. Depending on the size of the bottle and the amount of food, you can vary the degree of difficulty of your food dispenser. In the beginning, arrange for quick success (with a small bottle and a lot of food inside). Caution: this food dispenser is not firm to the bite. Your dog should not play unsupervised with it.

How do I get to the treat?
Tiffi tries to find it out.

A filled tube

Solid cardboard or plastic tubes are perfect for all kinds of treat games. Drill several holes into the sides of a lockable cardboard tube for instance. Put food into the tube, close the lid and lay it down on the ground. Your dog now has to move the tube with his muzzle or his paws so that the treats fall out through the holes.

Solid tubes without a lid can be filled with treats without drilling holes into the sides first. Your dog has to try to get to the treats inside by moving the tube.

Classical treat balls

Treat balls in all kinds of variations are part of the standard stock of most pet stores today. The right ball for your dog should be big enough that he can't take it into his mouth and swallow it. If you have a rather small dog the ball shouldn't be too big and bulky. Most models have an adjustable opening that can be adapted to the size of the treats and the desired degree of difficulty.

> **Tip**
> Especially when you have neighbours who are sensitive to noise and when your apartment is rather small remember, the softer the ball, the less noise it will produce when hitting furniture and walls.

Lara earns her food with the treat ball. Due to an adjustable opening the degree of difficulty can be varied.

Kimba is mystified: "What is this funny thing?"

"Let's approach it from the side. Hmmm, it smells good but there is nothing coming out. I'll try and push it a little ..."

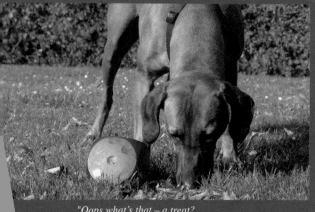

"Oops what's that – a treat? Ah, there it is!"

Beppo is very busy with the food skipjack.

The cube

It is hardly imaginable that the treat ball will ever become boring for your dog. Nevertheless, he will enjoy variety – and you probably will too. Food cubes are especially fun on grass or in large rooms covered with carpets. There you can move them easily and they don't make too much noise. It's not so easy for your dog to roll the cube and to make sure not to miss a treat falling out at the same time!

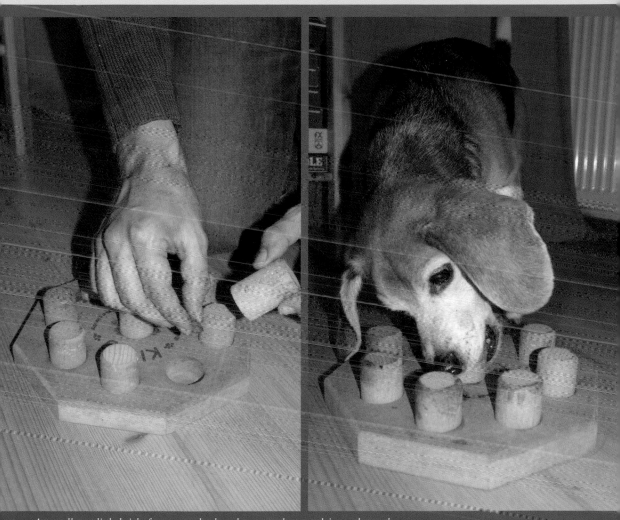

Asta pulls out little bricks from a wooden board to get to the treats lying underneath.

The food skipjack

Food dispensers that sit up again and again like a skipjack are popular with many dogs because of their unpredictable movements. When your dog has discovered the right strategy the food skipjack is applicable even in a small room.

Games to buy for mental acrobats

When searching for dog toys in pet stores not long ago the only thing that could be found was an enormous variety of balls and squeakers. Slowly but surely things are changing.

As mental stimulation is fashionable and good for dogs, clever games capture the market. With those games the dogs are facing different challenges. The dog that wants to get the desired treat for instance has to:

- pick up little plugged in wooden bricks to get to the treats lying underneath

- move around a slider with his paw to open containers underneath
- move a disc, or
- push food out of a labyrinth by moving a wooden spool

The games are not really cheap to buy but most of them are real highlights for all two- and four-legged game fans.

Lana has to push the treats out of a labyrinth by moving wooden spools.

That's where the treats are! Coda moves the sliders with his paws.

Photo: N Szabautzki

Chewing
makes you happy!

Chewing as a game for dogs? This might sound a bit strange at first but it is in fact a great occupational therapy that is really fun for the dog, easy to do and has a lot of positive side-effects.

Chewing is one of the dog's natural needs. It keeps his jaws and teeth in shape and for him it is at least as pleasurable as watching an exciting film or reading a good book is for us. A dog that gets enough opportunities to chew is more satisfied and even-tempered – and will probably use his teeth less on our furniture, shoes or carpets. Chewing furthermore is an ideal occupational therapy if

So much to choose from: Asta reviews an assortment of supplies for different chewing games.

you don't have enough time for joint activities with your dog occasionally. While you are occupied with other things, your dog also has something to do. Objects to chew on shorten the waiting time when your dog has to stay alone occasionally, and therefore are useful devices in preventing separation anxiety. You can also take along something to chew on when your dog accompanies you to another place, and this should keep him calm there.

Tips for chewing games
• Of course your dog should only get objects to chew on in healthy quantities.

In principle you can also use part of his daily meal for chewing games.

• Find out which objects your dog likes to chew an best, which ones he tolerates best, and which ones keep him occupied longest.

• If you don't want your dog to consume his aromatic chewing objects on the living room carpet, then take the chewing activities into another room or out to the garden (Caution, in late summer greedy wasps can spoil the chewing fun!). A big washable towel on your dog's favourite chewing spot saves the precious Persian carpet too.

• Safety comes first. In the beginning, don't leave your dog alone with objects to chew and snacks. Watch how he is handling them first. If he tends to destroy refillable chewing objects or to eat up the snack packaging, then he should only enjoy these while you are present. When staying alone he only gets the safe models.

• Make sure that your dog can chew undisturbed and unhurriedly. If you haven't trained taking away or exchanging objects yet, at first only give your dog objects to chew that he can consume in one go and that you don't have to take away from him again.

• If you have several dogs in your household chewing at the same time, consider having them in separate rooms to keep the atmosphere relaxed.

Things don't always go as harmonious as with Ronja and Tibor.
If in doubt, rather consider separate rooms for chewing activities.

Chewing objects as they are!

There's no easier thing: pizzle, rawhide, pigs' ears and so on are classic objects for chewing fun. You can give them to your dog as they are – and he will be occupied for quite a while. Try out different objects to chew before you store them in large quantities. Not every dog likes and tolerates them all. Also find out how long your dog is occupied with the different objects. By the way, opinions are divided on feeding real bones. In case of doubt ask your vet for advice!

Young dogs especially have a strong desire to chew. If they have the possibility to let off steam with permitted chewing objects, like Fredo has, chances are high that they will leave carpets or shoes alone. Photo. J. Hannemann

Natural rubber toys

Indestructible natural rubber toys rank right at the top of dogs' popularity lists. There are several shapes and models on the market such as cone-shaped ones or tubes and balls. They are hollow inside and can be stuffed with all kinds of goodies with any degree of difficulty. Whatever treats your dog is supposed to get, what is usually sensed within seconds becomes a long lasting chewing pleasure.

There are endless recipe variations for stuffing natural rubber toys. Give your fancy full scope, whether you stuff them with kibble, canned food, fruit (no grapes or raisins!), vegetables, yoghurt, cheese, dog biscuits or chews in any combination is your choice. Pros stuff cones and balls in different layers so that the dogs really have something to do.

Some chewing objects have grooves on the outside that can, for instance, be filled with dog toothpaste, cream cheese or cheese spread. Even air-dried cheese slices and soft flat chewing strips can be easily stuffed into the grooves (just squeeze them in between and break off the overlapping parts).

Chewing pleasure is as great for dogs as a murder mystery evening or a good book is for us. Ronja nibbles at a stuffed Kong®.

Carlos pitches into a stuffed chewing ball with his sharp puppy teeth. Especially when teething, young dogs really enjoy chewing. Photo: N. Szabautzki

Those toys are supposed to be especially appropriate for cleaning the teeth. In any event, your dog will have fun and be occupied with getting the food out of the grooves for a long time. Admittedly, the stuffing always leaves some marks on the floor. The towel underneath usually puts things right, or you must only give this kind of toy to your dog outside in the garden (remember the wasps!). Bear in mind that those dental toys with their thin grooves are often not as sturdy as the massive refillable chewing objects.

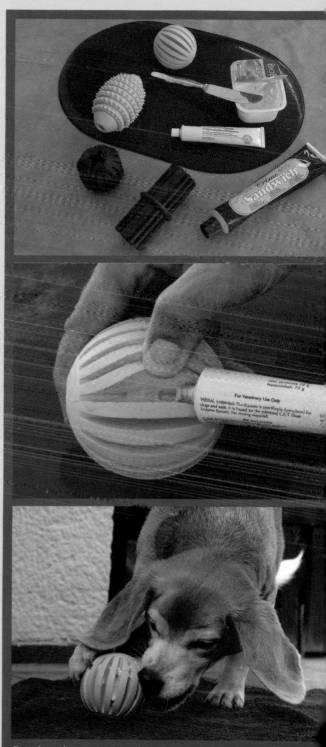

Dental toys have grooves on the outside that you can stuff with food or dog toothpaste. A towel put underneath or transferring the chewing pleasure out into the garden saves your precious carpets.

Tips
- Keep an eye on the quality of the toys. The higher price of some natural rubber toys often pays off. For instance, the original Kong® can be frozen or micro-waved (Caution, let it cool well before use!) and cleaned in the dishwasher.
- Choose a big enough chew toy so that your dog can't accidentally swallow it.
- Supervise your four-legged friend when chewing at first, before you leave him alone with the toy.

Recipe for Asta's chewing pleasure
- *Spread the inside of a natural rubber toy (or Kong®) with either cream cheese, peanut butter, cheese spread, pâté or liverwurst.*
- *Line the inside with some cheese slices.*
- *Then fill in any kind of kibble, canned food, fruit, vegetables, cooked potatoes, noodles, rice or dog biscuit.*
- *Close the opening with kibble or a dog biscuit.*

A good Kong® resists even the most severe attacks. Here Coda is working on a food stuffed Kong®.

Recipe for Coda's chewing pleasure
This is long lasting chewing fun for especially eager chewers! To get to the cooked content, the toy has to be worked hard by the dog. Therefore look out for the toy's sturdiness and good quality!
- *Mix kibble or dog biscuits with pieces of cheese and put into the natural rubber toy (Kong®).*
- *Put the toy into a cup and microwave it until the cheese has melted.*
- *Let it cool sufficiently and only give it to the dog when the content has cooled down completely!*

Don't put your toilet paper rolls into the waste paper anymore and in the future your dog will be very happy as you can easily make little lunch boxes of them.

Snacks and packed lunch

Why not let your dog nibble and tear a bit to get to his food? This makes it more exciting. You can easily pack part of his daily dry food in chewing objects, or give him the ready filled chew toys.

You can use newspaper, cardboard rolls, paper bags, wrapping paper or cardboard boxes. You can even wrap them in a piece of cotton cloth, for example, an old T-shirt or jeans. The degree of difficulty can be varied at will. In principle, only use packaging that can't harm your dog.

Having fun with
"Sit" – "Down" – "Come"

Nearly every family dog knows "sit", "down" and "come". For many people and dogs, these obedience exercises are a rather annoying duty and are performed with little enthusiasm from both sides. It doesn't have to be that way! A necessary evil can easily turn into fun and games that while away the time and include the whole family. Along the way, you and your canine friend can even benefit: dogs that have learned how much fun it is to work together with their owners are more obedient in an emergency!

For starters, create the right attitude

A good attitude is the ideal foundation for perfect teamwork. Furthermore you need your dog's attention. Only then is he receptive to something new. Your job, in this little game, is to make sure that your dog is relaxed and in a good mood and concentrating on you. Can you make him wag his tail? Does he look at you attentively? Anything that is fun is permitted. Try it out. Talk to your dog nicely, motivate him with a treat or carefully wave his favourite toy. See what brings the biggest success. Incidentally, you can integrate this little warm-up routine into all the games you play with your dog.

Coming back is fun!

Coming back reliably is one of the most important things in your dog's life. And honestly, isn't it wonderful when your four-legged friend rushes up to you with flying ears and shining eyes as soon as you call him? Make it fun out together!

"What's up?" Tiffi looks into the camera motivated and full of expectations – always ready for a new game!

That you shouldn't overly exhaust your dog with too fast sprints over a long distance goes without saying. Always end the game early enough – whilst your dog is still enjoying it!

Come and find me!

Turn the coming back into an exciting search game. Don't just call your dog from different rooms in your apartment but hide yourself, for instance, behind a door. That way your dog first has to look around to find you. Celebrate and reward him when he has discovered you. You can also play hide and seek on your walks.

Has she already smelled it? Liesel is searching for Maria who is hiding behind the door with a treat in her hand.

Ronja, Manuela and Anette are playing the coming back game outside. Ronja rushes back and forth between her two-legged friends on a field – and always gets a treat at the end.

Coming back game for singles

If you play and train alone with your dog, you don't have to do without the fun of the coming back game. This works best on a walk or in the garden.

- Call your dog when you are absolutely sure that he will come.
- When he has nearly reached you, throw his treats a few meters behind you. Your dog will rush on directly to collect the treats.
- That way he is in the ideal position for the next round a few metres farther on. He will certainly be waiting for even more of those tasty treats – the perfect opportunity to call him once more.
- Once again, you throw the rewards so far behind you that your dog has to run a few metres. And again he will be in the right position for another sprint back to you.
- Only play this game in short sessions. Otherwise you are taking a risk that your dog will get too wound up racing for the treats.

The treat lane

Are you and your dog enjoying the coming back games? Then the time is right for a new challenge. For the treat lane you have to motivate your dog so that he passes a few bowls filled with treats and comes straight-away when you are calling him.

Preparing the game:

- Provide two sorts of treats, one really attractive food (for instance sausage) and one that is not so sought-after (for instance biscuit or dried food).

Even those who are playing and training alone don't have to do without the fun of the coming back game.

Asta is never averse to a little snack. Still, she doesn't even look at the bowls with kibble in at all. The tempting sausage smells at the other end make the decision easy for her. When Asta has come back successfully a few times, her owner could gradually place the treat bowls closer to each other, call Asta from a greater distance or increase the number of bowls. Photos: Chr. Henke

- You need two bowls at first, and later on several. Sealable plastic boxes are ideal (for instance salad bowls from the super market) or jam jars.
- Drill a few holes in the lids. Put in some of the less attractive treats and close the lids.
- And now ideally ask a nice human assistant for some help.

And this is how it works:

- Your assistant holds your dog carefully or distracts him a little. Alternatively let your dog wait at the starting point.
- Now place the bowls in a wide lane, with the less attractive food to the left and right of you.
- Take the especially sought-after food into your hand. Get your dog's attention and call him.

Does your dog rush up to you without looking at the treat bowls? Congratulations, well done! Now you can gradually make the lane narrower or include a greater number of bowls.

Is it not working very well yet and is your dog running over to the bowls? No problem. As long as your dog is not an expert in opening plastic boxes (in which case you can still use jam jars with screw caps), he can't reward himself because the containers are closed. So you don't need to scold him, but try to get better yourself. Make the situation easier for your dog. Place the bowls farther apart and call your dog over a very small distance at first. When you and your tasty treats are quite close to your dog

Zito has a flying dog in him. When called, he runs up enthusiastically.

and the less attractive treats are far away, it will probably work at first go.

The flying dog

By now you should really be good at making your dog come running enthusiastically to you when called. Now why not integrate your coming back game into your daily routine? Can you motivate your dog to come running nearly every time you call him? This is a challenge that will earn jealous looks from other dog owners.

"Sit" and "down" in different places

Can your dogs do "sit" and "down"? You will probably have already trained him to do that frequently. But can your dog also do it when you are lying on your back or doing press-ups? And can he do it on a newspaper or a plastic bag? Does he sit down when you ask him to only by using your body language, or by using just a word without moving?

Tips for "sit and "down"

• If your dog cannot do "sit" and "down" yet, teach him to do so first. For this, consult a good, modern dog training book (see "Recommended reading" at the end of this book).

• As always, never push, pull or drag your dog into certain positions. Never lose your patience. Give all cues in a nice and friendly way.

• When your dog has completed the exercise successfully and has got his reward for it, let him go by giving a special cue (for instance "go" or "okay").

• The journey is the reward! It's unlikely, especially in the beginning, that "sit" and "down" in unfamiliar positions are successful at first go. A "sit" on the living room carpet can be a completely different exercise from your dog's point of view to a "sit" on a box or on the lawn in your garden. Now it's your job to split the exercise into little pieces. Let's say you want your dog to sit while you are lying on your belly under a blanket (and why not?). Visualise the structure of the exercise like a flip-chart:

1. First ask your dog to sit while you are in a normal position. Let's say you are standing in front of your dog. Your dog gets his reward and is allowed to stand up again (throw the treat to the ground next to your dog so that he has to stand up to pick it up).

2. Now you start to change the situation. First, put the blanket around your shoulders and give your familiar "sit" cue. Your dog is allowed to stand up afterwards.

3. Gradually bend your knees and keep repeating the sequence "sit" – reward – get up.

4. Do so until you reach the ground, at first on all fours, and then on your belly.

5. While practising, pull the blanket bit-by-bit over your head and reward the dog for every right reaction.

6. If it doesn't work just go back one step.

You can design nearly any other exercise in a similar way!

Strange positions

Try to make your dog sit or lie down, or fulfil another familiar exercise, from unusual positions. You can for instance:

• bend down on all fours

• lie on your back on your belly

• bend down and look at your dog through your legs

• be hidden under a blanket

• turn your back on your dog

- lift your arms up over your head
- be hiding behind a newspaper
- be sitting in the bathtub
- be lying on your bed or the sofa
- be holding a shopping bag in each hand

and many other things.

By the way, it takes several thousand repetitions before a dog is capable of fulfilling an exercise perfectly in different situations and despite all kinds of distractions!

When you want to make your dog sit or lie down from a strange position, you have to teach him to do so as with any other new exercise – in very small steps.

In this exercise, Sun learns that "sit" also means sitting down when Renate is lying on her belly in front of her, or lifting her legs up, lying on her back. Because Sun already knows this game, she is quickly successful. Make it easy for your dog in the beginning and change your body position step-by-step.

"Sit" and "down" criss-cross

You are probably using a certain word (for instance "sit") and a special gesture (for instance an upraised finger) to make your dog sit or lie down.

• Can you make your dog fulfil the exercise when you are not talking and only using your body language?

• And vice versa: Does your dog complete the exercise when you only use your voice without moving?

Try it out! Your dog will probably also have the fewest problems with the method of only using your body language. This is completely normal! Most dogs listen to their owner's body language rather than to the spoken word.

When you are able to communicate with your dog from this position, you are really good!

"Sit" and "down" everywhere!

Is your dog so confident that he also fulfils the familiar exercises in unknown places? And can you guide your dog into different positions without touching him? In this game, it's your job to make your dog sit or lie down, or fulfil other familiar exercises, in a wide variety of places, such as:

- on a box
- on a newspaper or a piece of paper
- right on top of a post-it note (with the sticky side facing the ground) or on a certain spot on a patterned carpet
- on a wall
- exactly on the edge of the kerb
- in unfamiliar rooms such as the garage or the attic
- on a plastic bag

A twofold challenge for Asta: She lies down enthusiastically just by hearing the word "down" – and all this on a tree trunk! This is working so well because Asta knows how to lie down on cue and also is an experienced and confident tree climber. Asta has learned both parts separately first – until the combination has turned into a new game. Photo: Chr. Henke

You should only make your dog sit or lie down where he feels comfortable. A "down" on top of sharp stones or a forced "sit" on a weird, rustling plastic cover (from your dog's point of view) would be unfair! After all, you both want to have fun!

Anette makes Zito sit down right in the middle of a hoop – of course without touching him.

Carlos does a "sit" on top of a concrete block and even during an exciting walk through the city. He actually can do it when Norbert is standing a little away from him.

Staying power

Is your dog already quite good at sitting or lying down on your cue and even remains in this position until you let him get up? Now you can include some funny distractions. While your dog is sitting or lying down:

- wave your arms
- jump up and down a few times
- open and close an umbrella (at first, of course, very carefully so that your dog doesn't get scared)
- turn around
- do press-ups
- and so on.

Only integrate as many distractions as your dog can handle and still be successful. If he gets up nevertheless, don't scold him, but think about what you could do to make him succeed. In the beginning, reward him for sitting or lying down at a simple stage and increase the distractions step-by-step.

Building bridges

When your dog enjoys sitting on a piece of cardboard, a small blanket or a doormat, and has also learned to stay there for a little while, you might also enjoy building bridges. You only need two similar pieces of cardboard. Alternatively you can, of course, also use two doormats, towels or blankets.

And this is how it works:

- At first, define a rather short distance with a starting point and an end.
- Place one of the pieces of cardboard at the starting point and make your dog sit on top of it, for instance.
- Then place the second piece of cardboard in front of the first one and let your dog swap position. He takes a few steps and sits down again.

Regardless of whether Christian is doing press-ups or jumping around on one leg with upraised arms, Mikel stays in a "down" position!

• Now you take away the one behind, place it in front of the one the dog is sitting on, and let your dog move forward again.
• Repeat these steps until you reach the end.

Can you reach the end without your dog leaving the bridge? As always, you are responsible for the success of the game. Make it easy for your dog! At first, choose a short distance and large pieces of cardboard and reward your dog with a piece of food for every "sit".

The loose lead

Isn't it relaxing to walk around with your canine friend on a loose lead? This doesn't only look nice, it is also much more comfortable (and healthier) for dog and owner than having a wheezing dog at the one end of a tight leash. How to teach walking on a loose lead in a nice and non-violent manner can be found in good, modern dog training books. Leash work games can also be a pastime in your joint play. Check out how good you are in handling your dog.

The fine cord

For this game you need a very special lead: it consists of a 2 meter long fine cord or a paper tear out!

Attach your special lead to your dog's collar or harness with a loose slip knot.

Jessi and Taja are building a bridge. Photos: D. Zünd

With a few buckets, little pylons or some chairs, you can easily set up a small slalom course in your living room or the garden. Do you manage to handle your dog well enough that you both complete the slalom course without breaking the cord? Anything that motivates your dog to stay by your side is permitted.

Game version for advanced players:

Can you manage to motivate your dog to follow you without a treat or a toy in your hand? Of course, he still gets a reward but from your pocket!

Egg-and-spoon race

Is the slalom course, with your special lead, rather boring for you and your dog? Then let's face the next challenge. First pick up a spoon or a small cup with a tennis ball on it. Try to complete the slalom course without breaking the cord or dropping the ball!

Tip

Take the spoon and your special lead into the same hand. That way you have one hand left to lure your dog into the right position with a treat or a toy.

The special lead breaks immediately when it is taut. Jasmin and Desmond start with the slalom course in the living room. With less distractions success is certain.
Photo: K. Schomburg

Your Garden as a Playground

Agreeable temperatures and sunshine make you feel like playing joint activities in the fresh air. Of course, you can take most of the games you are usually playing inside, out into the garden or a field when it's warm outside. But there are also a few occupational therapies that can be realised exclusively or at least especially well outside. Even the smallest piece of green offers enough space for fun and games with your dog. And if you want to, you can build a small mobile playground for your dog with little craftsmanship and at a low cost.

Tips for the perfect garden fun:

- You already know some of the games presented in this chapter as "Living room agility". But you and your dog have a bigger freedom of movement outside and you can use other equipment, and this is the point. In order to make it not too boring, not every exercise structure is described again. When you need more precise instructions on how, for instance, to make your dog run through a tunnel, jump over an obstacle or do a slalom, have a look in the chapter "Living room agility".

- Playing in the garden together is most fun when you observe the common rules: always adjust your activities to your dog's physical abilities; keep the sessions short; set your dog up for success; and be generous with rewards. Motivate your dog with treats or toys instead of pushing or pulling him around. Only use materials for your garden playground that your dog can't hurt himself with.

- The weather outside is not always ideal for movement games. When it is hot, take it slow and remove your activities to the shade. Remember to provide water for your dog!

- He who has worked a lot is allowed to have a nice rest afterwards! You will probably have no objections to a joint rest in a cosy place.

This is fun, too! Asta enjoys a joint sunbathe!

Space for high jumps

Would you like to set up a little obstacle course for your agile, jumping dog? No problem, this is possible even with little equipment.

Basic jumps

You definitely have what you need for building simple obstacles at home. You can for instance:

- place a flower box or a shelf between two garden chairs, or
- use two containers or upside down plastic boxes as side frames and lay a long pole on top

Can you make your dog jump over the obstacles?

Plastic flower boxes easily turn into a simple garden jump. It is easiest for the dog when the jumps are boxed in by poles or chairs to the sides.

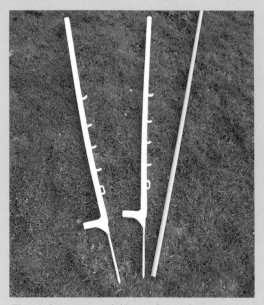

Electric fence posts and thin wooden or plastic poles can easily be used to build low-priced training jumps.

Self-made professional jumps

When you and your dog are enjoying obstacle courses, you can easily build your own mobile and, above all, low-priced training jumps. Four jumps provide the basic equipment, but you can also do a lot with one or two of them.

For each jump you will need:

- two electric fence posts from an agricultural store as side frames, and
- one pole of about 1 metre length (a thin plastic pole or a round wooden pole about 12 millimetres in diameter).

If you heat up the clamps of the posts with a hair dryer, you can bend them and mould them into clamps for your bar holders at different heights.

With your brand new training jumps you have many training and play possibilities.

Coda is a high achiever. Even in small gardens, there is enough space for a few jumps over the training obstacles.

- Move the jumps slightly and build-in angles.
- When your dog has got some practice, you can set up the jumps in interesting combinations, for instance: as a cross, as an open square, as a staircase or one next to the other in a line.
- Think about in which order you and your dog would like to take your little obstacle course.

Tip
The lower the jumps are at first, the easier it is for your dog. 30 centimetres for large dogs and 15 centimetres for small dogs are more than enough for the first jumping experiences.

A variation for advanced players: Meggan does the jumping square.

Tip
For very large dogs, the posts should be at least 1.40 meters high. You don't want your dog to be injured when he jumps very high and lands incorrectly. Also provide high enough side frames for the flower box jumps.

Start with a single jump:
- Begin right in front of the jump and make your dog jump over it with or without you.
- Gradually take a longer run.
- Run on your dog's left and right side.
- Approach the jump from different angles.

Then in a next step integrate two or more jumps:
- First of all, set up the jumps in a row so that your dog can jump over them without a change in direction.

Jumps as tests of courage

Wouldn't it be boring if you could only use your self-made jumps for a single purpose? This is how you turn them into an exciting test of courage:

- Place the bar as high as possible. Preferably attach it to the side frames so that it can't fall down.
- Attach several plastic strips or newspaper strips, for instance, to the bar.

How to motivate your dog to walk through a fluttering curtain was explained in the chapter on "Living room agility". If your dog is already an experienced obstacle

Kimba carefully walks through the fluttering curtain. Some treats scattered on the ground reward her courage.

Ronja does the bamboo stick weave poles. Photo: M. Schumann

jumper, make sure that he doesn't jump over the bar accidentally.

Weave poles

Weave poles and mobility exercises work best in a field. There you can easily push your poles into the ground and obtain a stable construction.

Basic weave poles

For the basic weave poles, just drill a few bamboo or plastic sticks from a do-it-yourself store into the ground.

Do-it-yourself professional weave poles

Those who like to do handicrafts could use several broomsticks (for small dogs halved broomstick are enough), paint them in different colours and screw a tent peg on each one of them.

> Remember:
>
> First lure your dog through the poles with a treat in your hand. If you want to expand the exercise, reduce the treats step-by-step so that the dog follows your empty hand and gets his reward afterwards. In the beginning, use two or three poles and add more of them gradually.

That is fun and looks good. Lara does the professional garden weave poles.

A set of bowling pins turns into a mobility exercise for Liesel

More mobility exercises

Of course, you can also include all kinds of objects into your mobility exercises in the garden. Let your dog circle the legs of your garden furniture or set up your children's plastic cones or little pylons in a slalom course.

Tunnels and hoops

Your children's crawl-through tunnel and all kinds of hoop jumps are great fun on the right surface and with enough space. With a bit of wood and craftsmanship, you can build a stable hoop stand yourself.

Independently, Sun runs through the tunnel. As a reward her ball is thrown for her.

How to introduce your dog to the tunnel or the hoop jump is explained in the chapter on "Living room agility". You pass through exactly the same steps in your garden training. Then you can additionally train:

- approaching the tunnel or hoop with a little run-up and energy
- running with your dog on your right side and then on your left side
- approaching the tunnel or hoop from different angles.

Living obstacles

Have you already done some gymnastics with your dog and used your body to form all kinds of obstacles? In your garden there is even more space for those activities. You can include jumps into your

Tip
You should stabilise your tunnel with a few sticks or poles stuck into the ground on both sides so that it can't wobble or roll away during fast movements or windy weather.

With a bit of imagination and craftsmanship, you can build beautiful garden obstacles like this hoop jump.

Yesterday bulky waste, today a challenge in your garden course! An old slatted child's bed frame becomes a special body awareness obstacle.

Tests of courage and co-ordination games

Use the space in your garden for all kinds of tests of courage and co-ordination games that will train your dog's body awareness and are good for his self-confidence!

Fantasy obstacles for body awareness training

Take a look into your garage, cellar, attic or summerhouse. You will definitely find things there that you can use for all kinds of co-ordination exercises. For instance:

• a wooden ladder
• several car tyres
• plant poles, or
• an old slatted frame

can be placed on the ground and your dog allowed to step over it slowly and with concentration.

Outside there is more space for energetic run-ups and high jumps. Always adjust your living obstacles to your dog's abilities and make absolutely sure that he is enjoying the exercises.

programme, set up several people as a living obstacle course, or take an energetic run.

Kimbu steps carefully through plant poles.

A whole lot of new impressions: Zito walks across the fumble course.

The fumble course

Have you already introduced your dog to all kinds of different surfaces when doing "Living room agility"? Then you can now set up a whole fumble course with different elements. You can, for instance, use rustling plastic covers, unfolded newspapers, a plastic or metal tray, a door mat, a piece of Styrofoam, a flat plastic box, a piece of carpet, a piece of cardboard paper and many other things. Can you make your dog walk across the different surfaces?

It doesn't have to be the whole course at once: Ronja makes herself familiar with the individual elements first.

Tip

It's likely that doing the whole course at once will involve your dog in quite an effort at the beginning, in which case, just lead him across the individual elements diagonally.

The dog teeter

The wobble board balance exercise in the living room can turn into a big dog teeter outside.

- Place a log, a rolled up towel or an old ball with little air left inside under a shelf or a non-slip board.
- The less the board is wobbling in the beginning, the easier it is for the dog.

- Reward him generously for all activities on and with the teeter, for touching the teeter with a paw, for stepping onto it carefully, for making it topple over and so on.

Asta and her dog teeter: whenever she makes it topple over by herself she gets a reward. Photos: C. Henke

Rolling adventure

Do you have a bicycle trailer, a skateboard or a little wagon? You can integrate all these things into your games! Of course you shouldn't just put your dog on the vehicle and push it around. This might look funny, but your dog probably wouldn't enjoy it all. Far from it - it is more likely that he will get scared and fed up with joint activities for a while. Therefore you need a little common sense:

- At first, choose a vehicle that you don't have to lift your dog onto, for instance, a flat transport wagon or a bicycle trailer or (for small dogs) a skateboard.
- Make sure that the vehicle can't start moving suddenly. Hold onto it tightly or block the wheels.
- Motivate your dog to mount the vehicle now. If your dog is very nervous give him a reward just for lifting a paw to make the first step.

A skateboard on the lawn is a good start for a rolling adventure. It only moves slightly and doesn't roll away suddenly, Nelly is rewarded for having the heart to take the first step.

- Let your dog get on and off a few times without moving the vehicle.
- Make your dog stay a little longer on the vehicle. Give him several treats.
- Now carefully move your vehicle. Re-

ward your dog at once when he stays down or stands still calmly.
- The vehicle's first little move can gradually be turn into pushing or pulling over a short distance later on.

Here a flat transport wagon turns into a dog vehicle. In order not to scare the four-legged passenger, the wheels should be blocked at first. A blanket makes it comfortable and non-slippery.

Taja is rewarded for mounting the fixed wagon first.

The wagon is only moved a tiny bit when she has made herself comfortable and is relaxed.

When the wagon is moving, Taja is rewarded with treats for being so brave. Photos: D. Zünd

The pushcart game is only for advanced teams. Your four-legged friend has to trust you totally and you have to understand his languageas well. As soon as you recognise the slightest discomfort, choose another game.

Zito knows exactly the activities with Anette that are always fun. He happily jumps into the pushcart with a blanket inside.

"Hey, it's nice here!" A treat reinforces his positive sentiment.

"Let's go then!" It's obvious that Zito is enjoying his adventure. Photos: R. Heymann

Tiffi loves water: she jumps into the small water basin enthusiastically and is fishing and plunging for treats. If your dogs prefers to fish for the food from outside the basin, that's fine, too!

Water games

Outside in the garden, your dog might enjoy some rather splashy activities. Throw a handful of kibble into a big bowl filled with water and let your dog go fishing for it. You can also spread out a plastic cover, pour out some water on it and guide your dog across the refreshing footbath.

When your dog takes a bath, he should be doing it voluntarily! If you put him into the water it's no fun for him anymore.

The digging corner

Dogs have their own idea of garden and spare time arrangements. While you are lovingly cultivating your flower bed or en-joying the sunshine, reading a book on your deck chair, your dog might just be digging a huge hole into your lawn in order to bury his chewing bone. In cases such as this, a digging corner might help. This can be a certain part of a flower-bed, or a sandbox, or a sectioned-off piece of lawn. There your dog can let off steam to his heart's content. Introduce the digging corner to your dog by burying several treats or a toy while he is watching you, and encourage your canine friend to go and search for the hidden treasures.

Busy Fredo. He enjoys his digging corner in the garden and the flower bed are safe. Photos: J. Hannemann

The mixed course

There definitely isn't enough space for this in your living room. You can set up nearly all of the different garden agility obstacles as a little course. For instance, combine the tunnel with a jump, include a few co-ordination exercises and finish off the whole thing with a funny treat search in the water bowl. The possibilities are almost endless.

Your dog is certainly always the winner in your course! It doesn't depend on speed. Your dog should first of all feel comfortable and be successful – and this is mainly your job!

Anything else?

Everyone has different objects at home, every garden looks different, and therefore no garden course will look like another! Try out something new now and again. Your dog will be thrilled!

That's fun! Many different challenges are set up for Tiffi on a meadow.

You can make great things out of these: Asta and Coda with the equipment in their garden playground.

Everyone has different objects at home. Two large plastic vats from the stables turn into a fantasy obstacle for Kira.

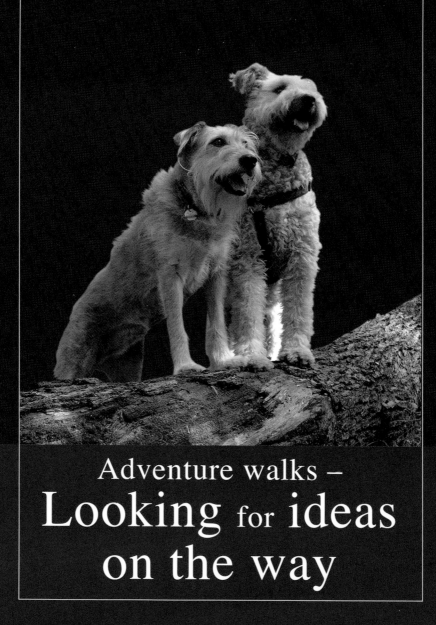

Adventure walks –
Looking for ideas on the way

Keeping your dog occupied doesn't have to be time consuming. A little programme of funny activities can easily be integrated into your regular walks. Whether you are walking in the woods, in the fields, or in the middle of the city – with a little bit of creativity you can provide something for your four-legged friend in any environment. This way even the shortest of walks becomes an adventure for your dog.

Joint activities on your walks don't only provide variety but are also very useful. You will notice that your dog pays much more attention to you when you include little surprises into your walks regularly. It will be less likely that your dog undertakes trips on his own when you become more interesting to him. When your dog is not allowed to run off lead, usually because of his strong hunting instincts, a little occupational therapy on your walks is even better for him.

For most of the games, a lead won't hold you up at all and you can provide a valuable alternative activity for your dog.

Open air course along the way

Walk along your daily route with a completely different view. You will suddenly

---

Tips for the open air course

• Your dog's safety always comes first. Obstacles that your dog could slip off of, fall down from, or get hurt by, are not suitable for your open air course!

• When you are walking cross-country remember nature! Inform yourself about which paths you're allowed to walk on and which areas you may enter.

• In order that the new challenges really turn into a special pleasure for your dog, the following rules apply as usual: never pull or push your four-legged friend; and lead him into the right position, preferably without any body contact, just with a cue or a treat.

• The stranger the obstacles, the bigger the challenge for your dog. Immediately reward the tiniest attempts at managing a test of courage.

• Outside the distractions from numerous stimuli like smells or sounds are much higher than in your house or your garden. Therefore start with very easy games and especially attractive rewards.

There are loads of game opportunities along the way. Here a knobbly branch turns into an adventure for Coda.

realise that there are loads of interesting things to your left and to your right that you can integrate into your game and occupation programme. Set up your own open air course!

Balancing act

Your dog can balance perfectly over low walls, non-slippery and stable tree trunks or narrow bridges. As long as your dog isn't used to this exercise, choose especially wide and low natural gangways. Make sure that your dog doesn't slip off.

In the forest you have tree trunks, in the city concrete blocks. Marius tries them out. Photo: M. Meyerolbersleben

> **Tip**
> Stacks of wood used as jungle gyms can become very dangerous. Especially the ones piled up mechanically to a height of over 2 metres that are not made to be climbed. Particularly after longer rainy periods, such stacks can start to slip by themselves. That makes several tonnes of moving weight …

*Coffey especially enjoys climbing opportunities along the route. Here she has chosen a hydrant. For beginners, non-slippery platforms are better.
Photo: M. Meyerolbersleben*

Non-slippery and stable, thick tree trunks are made for a balancing act. Queenie thinks so as well.

Platforms and other climbing opportunities

Make your dog climb up a tree trunk or a concrete block and reward him for it. If you like, you can also teach your dog to run to the next tree trunk or concrete block on his own and climb up on cue:

- It's easiest for your dog when, in the beginning, you keep using the same platform for training.
- Lure your dog onto the trunk or block a few times in a row and reward him there.
- Then think about which verbal cue you want to use for this exercise in the future, for instance "climb". Give the cue immediately before you lure your dog onto the platform from now on.
- Whilst you were situated right next to your four-legged friend at first, now you move a little farther away literally step-by-step and let your dog reach his aim on his own. With a little bit of training, you will soon be sending him to the platform from a few metres distance.

When stumps, boulders or concrete blocks become part of your open air course more often, you will recognise that your dog automatically starts watching out for them.

Higgledy-piggledy!

Now that you and your dog have probably tried out a few jumps over your self-made obstacles in the house or in your garden, check out how many of those obstacles you can find along the wayside. The forest especially is a good source. Try, for instance, to make your dog jump over a fallen tree trunk. But don't make it too high and make sure that your dog can't get hurt while jumping and landing.

This combination was situated on a picnic area – and turned into an obstacle for Sun.

Carlos passes underneath a bicycle stand.

Co-ordination exercises with Asta and the branches.

Your dog can also be a "high achiever" when he chooses an exercise at ground level. You can, for instance, make him crawl underneath some branches or roots in the woods or make him pass underneath a bench, a gate or a bicycle stand.

Co-ordination exercises on your way

Body awareness, concentration and mobility can be trained along the way. There are loads of opportunities. Lead your dog slowly over fallen branches and thin tree trunks. If you like to, you can set up your own obstacles with a few sticks or guide your dog through a winding stick labyrinth.

Round and round it goes!

All kinds of trees, hay bales, flower tubs, poles or street lamps can easily be turned into slalom elements that your dog can negotiate together with you or on his own. Even if there are not enough elements for a whole slalom course (for example a single pole), you can still let your dog circle it in both directions. How this is trained is explained in the chapter "Living room agility".

> **Tip**
> It's especially fun when you are able to send your dog over to circle a tree or a pole with only a little gesture. Guide your dog around the pole from nearby a few times and increase the distance between your starting point and the pole gradually. With a little practice, you will soon be able to make your dog surround any tree or pole in your proximity with only a little gesture.

There are slalom elements everywhere.

Missie likes to take a bath in the shallow stream. Other dogs are more sceptical and should be introduced to water carefully.

- Take a treat and place it on a stone or in the water so that the dog only has to put one paw into the water to reach it.
- When he has managed to do this a few times successfully, you can increase the challenge a little. Now, to get to the treat, he has to put two paws in the water and later all four of them. And then at some point, the treat is even placed so that he has to walk a few steps in shallow water at first and then in the deeper part later on.

Adventures at the waterside

Water is a paradise for all game fans. Whether it's a puddle, a trickle, a stream or even the sea – you and your dog can have a lot of fun there.

Bathing challenge

How do you make your dog take a bath? Where water rats don't see any problems, dogs that are afraid of water might not be so happy at first. What you shouldn't do, of course, is to just take your dog and put it in the water. This will definitely not lead to your dog taking a bath voluntarily. Let him find out about it on his own:

- Start training at a still and shallow puddle or a narrow trickle. The water should only be a few centimetres deep.

Asta is usually afraid of water, but when a small trickle turns into a treat-slide, she can't resist anymore and enjoys the tracing. Photo: Chr. Henke

Treat tracing

When your dog has the heart to walk in shallow water, you can send him to do treat tracing. This works best in a shallow stream or trickle with little current. (Ed's Note: This should not be attempted in fast flowing or deep streams.) Just put a few floating treats (for example kibble or thin dog biscuits) into the water while your dog is watching and let them be carried away by the current. Your dog will probably start running to catch and eat up the treats. As a nice alternative, for toy junkies, you can use a rubber duck instead of treats.

Bridges and catwalks

Where there are streams and rivers you will probably also find bridges and fords. Crossing them can become an adventure for your dog especially when they are a bit unsteady or when your dog can see the run-

A short break with a calming effect: Spencer sniffs for some treats in a pile of leaves during an exciting walk through the city.

ning water through the chinks. As usual, never force your dog. Join him while walking over the bridge, make sure that he is safe and reward him generously for every test of courage passed.

Coda is an experienced balancing expert and wouldn't mind jumping into the shallow water if necessary. Always adapt your activities to your dog's abilities!

Rummaging and searching games

Surprise your dog with regular rummaging and searching games on your walks! Being together with you becomes even more interesting for your dog then – and the likelihood that he prefers joint activities to going on a sniffing and hunting trip on his own are high!

Foraging for treats

Many search games are already known from the chapter on "Sniffing games for super-noses". Integrate them into your daily walks as a nice little game on the way, as an attractive reward for coming back, or as a relaxing exercise in exciting situations. Think about even more variations. For instance hide the treats in a big pile of leaves, bury them in the snow or on the beach.

Hide and seek

What you might have already tried in the house works even better outside. You hide behind a tree or bush, your dog searches for you - and is generously rewarded with treats or play for being successful.

And this is how it works:

- If your dog has already learned to stay in one place on cue, then you can easily play this game on your own. If not, a human assistant who can look after the dog while you are hiding for help.

- At first let your dog watch while you are hiding, having treats or his favourite toy with you.

- Your dog will of course try to get to you quickly as soon as you call him. Therefore give him a reward immediately!

- Later on you can set up the game so that your dog can't see exactly where you are hiding. With a little bit of practice, your dog will soon enjoy searching quite large areas in order to find you. By the way, this is how search dogs are trained. For search

Missie. as a skilled search and rescue dog, is an expert in playing searching games. Any family dog can do what she is showing us here.

and rescue dog Missie, finding a missing person is nothing more than playing hide and seek. She has learned that it pays off to look out for people and she knows that she only deserves her reward (in this case a toy) when she barks at her "victim" persistently.

Sniffing walks

Having fun on a walk doesn't automatically have to involve a lot of action. Sniffing exciting and interesting smells is much more profitable for many dogs than, for instance, throwing a ball endlessly or going on extensive jogging tours. Invite your dog on a sniffing walk alone, or together with his four-legged friends.

Sniffing and exploring

If you go for a walk with your dog in the morning before leaving for work, you probably recognise this situation. You want to offer him enough exercise, but don't have a lot of time to do so, so you rush ahead and your dog can't really take his time investigating all those interesting smells along the way. You are probably also using the same routes in your everyday life that you and your dog already know inside out. Then it's time for a little exploratory fun!

Take your time on your walks and let your dog sniff his environment to his heart's content. Investigate new places with him regu-larly. For our dogs, this is a welcome change. They receive many impressions that they have to deal with and that make their brains work hard.

By the way, environmental exploration is used in modern behaviour therapy to strengthen self-confidence and as prevention against anxiety and aggression problems.

Tips for exploratory walks

- Leave your familiar paths regularly. Investigate new paths, out in the open or explore your housing area thoroughly. Even visiting a restaurant, a walk through the city, using an elevator, going on a trip by train or walking through an underpass can be an adventure for your dog.

- But don't overdo things. For dogs living in the country, visiting a shopping street in a large city will probably be way too much, and even for a city dog visiting the annual fair can turn into a bad trip.

- In unfamiliar situations the leash gives the dog security. It should be long enough (about 3 metres are best) and be kept slack as much as possible. Ideally your dog will be wearing a harness instead of a collar, as being pulled by the neck reduces the pleasure considerably and causes tension and headaches.

- In any new situation you should be completely devoted to your dog. Avoid agitation and rushing. Take your time and have a break sitting on a park bench and observing what's going on around you. An attractive treat every once in a while contributes to high spirits.

- As with all of the games remember when going out for an exploratory walk, less is more. The more exciting the new environment is, the shorter you should stay there. Also take into account that you will need more time for new paths than during a normal walk.
- You can also increase the exploratory fun factor on your daily walks. Just give your dog more time to inhale smells. Many dogs are happy about a little more tolerance on the lead and a patient owner, who allows them to sniff an interesting smelling blade of grass.
- Make sure that your dog gets enough rest after and between your exploration activities. That way he can go over experiences and you don't overwhelm him.

Reading the newspaper is very important! Carlos takes a look at who has been here before.

"What is this?" Fascinated, but still a little unsure, Spencer explores the fountain.

A harness and a long slack leash provide the perfect basic equipment for a relaxing exploratory walk.

Take your time. From time to time, just letting things pass by should be part of your exploration adventures, too.

- By the way, you should also have a bag to remove your dog's faeces with you in your basic equipment.

Sniffing in a group is even more fun

You probably want to make sure that your dog establishes friendly contact with other dogs. Meeting nice dogs is also important for a satisfied and happy life for your dog. Nice and calm exploratory walks in a group of dogs and people are perfect and also a highlight in your dog's daily routine. This is even often okay for dogs that have problems in a group of other dogs playing wildly. It is fascinating to see how the dogs are communicating without interacting directly with each other, as for instance when playing. They sniff together, pee together and sometimes also run a few metres together. Even on a leash and with a little distance between each other, such joint activities are possible.

Tips for a harmonious walk with your four-legged friends:
- When you meet with other dog people to go for a walk and the dogs are not yet familiar with each other, then just give them a little more space at first. That way you effectively avoid the tension and excitement within the dogs turning into a riot. When the dogs are supposed to run free, only let them off the leash when people and dogs are already moving and the initial excitement has calmed down a little bit.

- Please do not throw balls, sticks or other toys when walking with other dogs. This often turns into aggression and trouble within the group. When there are food aggressive dogs participating, you should also be careful about giving the dogs treats.
- It doesn't always have to be a large group of dogs. Many dogs can't cope with mass-events. They are much happier about a walk with their best dog friend.
- When you meet a strange dog on your walk, react carefully. Call back your dog first and talk to the owner of the other dog to see if and how the dogs can meet. If this is not possible, walk in a little – and in dog language nonconfrontational - curve together with your dog, instead of approaching the other dog head-on and passing it very close.
- By the way this is also courteous when you are meeting a strange dog while you are out with your dog on your own!

To these two four-legged friends, joint sniffing experiences are much more popular than wild play.

Photo: B. Laser

And what comes next?

Now you have reached the last pages. Maybe you are just sitting comfortably on your couch, your dog lying beside you or at your feet. Maybe you have tried out some of the games in the meantime and had fun together.

It would be wonderful if you and your dog had caught the game virus. You will recognise being infected at the time when new ideas appear in your mind's eye on your walks, when clearing out the attic, or when sorting empty packages after shopping. Your dog will be delighted!

When you and your dog have just discovered how much fun joint activities can be then playing together will probably make you want more. Maybe you would like to teach your dog a few tricks, continue train-

Maybe you will invent another gambling machine?
Photo: S. Putz

There are lot of books on training and occupational therapies for your dog nowadays. Thanks to clear instructions, many ideas can be worked on easily at home. You will find a small assortment of recommended dog literature at the end of this book.

Maybe you can also get input from a nearby trainer or would like to join a dog club with your dog? Then you should make sure that you choose a good one where dog- and people-friendly training is taken seriously. You and your dog will feel most comfortable and even learn the most where dogs and people are handled with respect and trainers do without yelling and violence.

But don't forget, sometimes less is more! Training shouldn't turn into spare time stress. Leave enough time and space for calm hours with your dog and take your time.

ing "important" exercises with more fun, or take a deeper look into one of the dog sports.

Maybe you would like to teach your dog a few tricks?

Whatever you are doing: Take your time! Photo: J. Hannemann

By the way, while your dog is lying next to you satisfied and happy, there might still be someone who is bored - maybe your cat? Cats also enjoy little challenges in their daily routine and love joint activities. Many of the games described in this book can also be played with cats – maybe in a slightly different way. Have a nice time!

Your dog is satisfied but your cat is still bored? Photo: B. Laser

Cats also enjoy playing together. Don't forget them! Photo: B. Laser

Photo: J. Hannemann

Recommended reading

Understanding dogs

Jean Donaldson
The Culture Clash
James & Kenneth Publishers, 1997

Turid Rugaas
On Talking Terms with Dogs:
Calming Signals
Qanuk Ltd, 2005

Dog Training

Pamela J. Reid Ph.D.
Excel-Erated Learning
James & Kenneth Publishers, 1996

Terry Ryan
Games People Play …
to Train Their Dogs
Legacy by Mail, 1996

Terry Ryan
Life Beyond Block Heeling
Legacy, 1996
Deborah A. Jones Ph.D.
Click 'n' Sniff
Howln Moon Press, 2001

Sarah Whitehead
Puppy Training for Kids
Thalamus Publishing, 2001

Peggy Tillman
Clicking with your dog:
Step-by-Step in Pictures
Sunshine Books, 2001

Pamela Dennison
The Complete Idiot's Guide
to Positive Dog Training
Alpha Books, 2003

Fun & Games

Mary Ray, Justine Harding
Dog Tricks: Fun and Games
for Your Clever Canine
Hamlyn, 2005
Gerilyn J. Bielakiewicz
The Only Dog Tricks Book You'll
Ever Need: Impress Friends, Family
and Other Dogs!
Adams Media Corporation, 2005